Preeti Shenoy  authors in India. Having written on varied themes and life experiences, she is also on the Forbes longlist of the most influential celebrities in India. Her books have been translated into several languages.

She has been awarded the 'Indian of the Year' award for 2017 by Brands Academy for her contribution to Literature. She has also received the Academia Award for Business Excellence by the New Delhi Institute of Management. She is the recipient of the '100 Young Indian Women Achievers Award' in the Powerful Leader category. She has given talks in many premier educational institutions such as IITs and IIMs, and corporate organisations like KPMG, Infosys and Accenture. She is also an artist specialising in portraiture and illustrated journalling.

Also well-known for her poetry and short stories, her recent book *Love A Little Stronger* is a collection of true stories and learnings from her own life. She has a very popular blog and also writes a weekly column in *The Financial Chronicle*.

Her massive online following only goes to show how popular she is! Her other interests are travel, photography and yoga.

Love
A Little Stronger

*A collection of true stories and learnings
from the author's life*

PREETI SHENOY

Srishti
PUBLISHERS & DISTRIBUTORS

SRISHTI PUBLISHERS & DISTRIBUTORS
Registered Office: N-16, C.R. Park
New Delhi – 110 019
Corporate Office: 212A, Peacock Lane
Shahpur Jat, New Delhi – 110 049
editorial@srishtipublishers.com

First published by
Srishti Publishers & Distributors in 2018

This is a work based on the author's experiences and life-learnings.

The author asserts the moral right to be identified as the author of this work.

Printed and bound in India

For my Father.

"Death is nothing at all.
I have only slipped away to the next room.
I am I and you are you.
Whatever we were to each other,
That, we still are."

— Henry Scott Holland

Contents

Introduction

What you are holding in your hands right now, is a very special book. It was more than ten years ago that I first wrote it. I never expected it to get published. I never thought there would be anyone other than me who would actually be interested in reading about little snippets from my daily life.

I had just lost my father and the only solace I found was in writing, and in my art. I poured out my soul, my grief, my longing, my understanding on life, and anything that I felt, into words. I wasn't even thinking about a book, much less thousands of people reading it. I didn't expect many to find inspiration from these true personal anecdotes.

But over the years, thousands have written to me saying that they loved it and that they could relate to what I have written.

A lot has changed since then. My children, who were little at the time of writing this, are adults now. Not only have they grown up, but as a writer, I have grown too.

When a reader picks up this book for the first time, the picture they get is a different one from what my reality is now. Since what you read at present is a version many years in my past, my publishers and I felt that it was time to make some changes.

In this book, I have included new stories, and made changes to many of the old ones. And after reworking it, we felt that the old title (*34 Bubblegums and Candies*) does not fit this version.

It was a joy for me to reflect, go down memory lane, and pick those which stood out, which made me learn something, which helped me grow.

This book is full of incidents from daily life. Often it is these small moments in the mundane of routine, which stand out, which make life worth living.

To those of you who are wondering about the old title (*34 Bubblegums and Candies*), I thought I would include the preface which appeared there which explained the title. (Incidentally, a friend pointed out that the plural of Bubblegum is Bubblegum. But word-hunter and many other sites say that Bubblegums is right, and hence I have let it be, because we can always count our bubblegums, can't we? Just like we count our blessings!)

Here's the preface of my first book.

It is only in fairytales that there are happy endings and the hero always wins. Real life is rarely like that. It is mostly imperfect. There are times when some things happen that are so embarrassing that you wish you had the powers to escape like Houdini; or you could change things with the flip of a switch like changing channels when you don't like a TV programme. No such luck. You just have to grin and bear it. But the good thing is that no matter what it is, it always ends. Just like candies that melt and fade and the bubblegum that you spit out when you are done with it.

When I mentioned the title of this book to a friend he said, 'Sounds interesting. Really interesting – but why Candies and Bubblegums?'

'Because, there are incidents that make you ponder and make you want to think and maybe re-think. Like chewing a bubblegum. Then there are others spiked with doses of humour, that make you laugh and leave you with a feel-good sensation. Just like eating a candy,' I explained.

He liked that.

Most of the incidents described in this book happened to me, and some of them to my friends. You may even relate to certain incidents and see yourself in some of them!

They just demonstrate that no matter how bad a day you have had, and no matter how hopeless the situation that you are in looks right now, things always change. Always. It is just a matter of time.

If you think you have had a bad day, just delve into the candy jar. And if you are in a mood to muse and ponder, help yourself to a bubblegum.

I have collected 18 candies and 16 bubblegums from my life, in this book. But, what is a candy to me, might be a bubblegum to you. It is for you to decide which is what — and we all know how deceptive it can be. Just like those sweet colourful balls that seem like candy, but when you bite and chew, they surprisingly turn into bubblegum! Or that bubblegum which suddenly has sweetness oozing out from its centre again, just when you thought that the juicy bit was over.

Each morning when you open your eyes, you are gifted 86,400 seconds to make a difference. And that by itself is worth celebrating!

In this refreshed version, I have tried to include all the stories that give you hope, make you think, touch you in some way, make you laugh, or at the very least, make you smile.

I have also included articles I have written which answer the questions that I get asked over and over again, about writing, blogging, things I have learnt and such. It is in the last section of this book.

I do hope you enjoy reading this book, as much as I have enjoyed writing it and putting it all together.

All the stories that appear here are true. Some names have been changed.

Thank you so much for reading this.

With love,

Preeti Shenoy
February 2018

THE PARENT TRAP

Your children are not your children.
They are the sons and daughters of Life's longing for itself.
They come through you but not from you,
And though they are with you yet they belong not to you.

– Kahlil Gibran

My special friend

Many of us have a friend who is more than just a friend. It is a relationship that is so much more than what can be defined by mere words, a relationship that cannot be fitted into slots built by the norms which society lays down. It is a relationship that you treasure and it makes your life richer, more meaningful and happier. You treasure it. You wonder what you would be if that person wasn't in your life anymore. You think about life without them and you cannot imagine it. I am no different.

Let me call him "K". I will not give you his name, for the obvious and not-so-obvious reasons.

K has always been a part of my life, ever since I can remember. Despite the vast age gap between us – he was so much older than me – we got along really well. The age difference between us never really bothered us. K looked so much younger than his age. He had the energy of a man half his age, and the maturity of a man twice his age. He was that rare, perfect combination. He was also extremely fit, tall and handsome, with a very striking presence.

He was an excellent swimmer. He was the one who taught me how to swim, when I expressed the desire to learn. He would splash water really hard on me with a swift repetitive movement of his hands and join my delighted peals of laughter when I got completely caught in a water jet created by the sheer power of his hands.

We were like children when we went to the beach. K could run really fast, and I would try to catch up with him, running as fast as my legs could carry me. I never succeeded. When I could go on no more, sweating and panting, I would stop and call out to him. He always laughed and said, 'You have to try harder. Never give up!'

I loved him with all my heart. And I think he knew it too – but we never spoke about it. When I was a gawky teenager trying to find my footing in life, K was there with gentle understanding. After all, he was a man, and here I was, dealing with only silly boys. He listened when I talked. Really listened. I could talk to him about almost anything, including boyfriends. I think he knew exactly whom I had crushes on. He was always polite and nice to them. I chatted with him about them.

K always encouraged me to reach my full potential. It is only because of his encouragement that I have several academic degrees today. He loved all my paintings and even when others thought they were just mediocre, K would always say they were brilliant. I don't think he ever lied to me. He sincerely believed what he said because he could not even draw a straight line, let alone paint. And funnily enough, his belief helped me become better – not just in academics, art or sports, but also as an individual.

K was already married when he came into my life. He adored his wife and I appreciated the way he took care of her. I hoped the guy I married would treat me the same way.

K was there when I got married. It was no surprise that I had chosen to marry a man like K. My husband understood my special relationship with K, and if he was jealous, he never showed it. In fact, K and he became good friends and got on really well.

K visited us whenever he could. He visited us when both my children were born and there were many trips in between too, when we spent a lot of time together. My children loved hanging out with K.

Life now took us in different directions. We were in different cities, yet most mornings, after my husband left for work, and after my children went to school, the first thing I'd do was call K. He was such a positive individual. I've never heard him say one bad thing about anyone the whole time that I have known him. K had an infectious laugh, a vivacious spirit and just talking to him made me feel so much better.

When I moved cities, I wanted K to visit me. It had been five whole months since I settled down in the new city, and he didn't even know what my new place was like, I complained. He agreed after a bit of persuasion and booked his plane tickets. I waited for him, counting down the days till I saw him.

I imagined us having long talks in my garden. I made a list of all the places we would go to. I had a lovely little garden with a lawn and I thought about how much K would enjoy sitting here with his morning cup of coffee and his newspaper. I had also set up a hammock on my terrace, and I pictured K lying in my hammock, gazing at the stars. (I have fond memories of philosophical discussions with him, under the stars, during another time). 'Not long, not long,' I kept telling myself in eager anticipation. I planned a trip to the airport to pick him up.

Then, out of the blue I got a phone call saying that K was dead. He had had a massive cardiac arrest. It was like a very bad nightmare coming true. I couldn't believe it. This was what happened in the movies. How could this even be? It left me frozen. Numb. Speechless. I didn't know it then, but it would take me a lifetime to recover. It would forever tinge all my happy moments with sadness. It would alter the way I looked at life.

You see, K was not only my special friend, he was also my dad.

John Cena versus Daddy

It was fall and we were living in the UK at that time. There was a cold nip in the air outside, with winter just setting in. The trees were bare and it was getting darker, earlier. One of the things my children loved to do during those days was have long conversations with me about anything that struck their fancy.

It brought back memories of similar conversations that I used to have with my father when I was a child.

'Dad, would you rather be a dead emperor or a living beggar?' I would ask. It was one of my favourite questions to ponder over.

'A dead emperor,' my father would answer with no hesitation.

'Why?' I would ask.

'Because, it meant he had led a great life, which was why he was an emperor,' my father would justify.

I would then say, 'But dad, he is dead!'

My father would reply that everybody had to die some day and a meaningful existence, where you are of use to somebody, is what makes life worth living. I would then argue that I would rather be a living beggar, as it meant I still had a chance to change my life. I would expostulate that it was better to be alive, as it meant you could do something, accomplish your goals. You also had a chance to change your life starting this very minute.

My father would always listen to my theories and arguments. He never got tired of questions like these which I would come up with, at very regular intervals. He never said that he was busy (which he was) for such hypothetical questions and we chatted away many hours, pondering on the what-ifs and life's deeper meaning. I treasured the hours spent in conversation with my father.

I carried on this tradition with my children and always encouraged them to have dialogues with me. They would bring up whatever they were obsessed with in that phase of their life. One of the things that my son loved, like most other ten-year-old boys, was watching *World Wrestling Federation* fights. He knew the names of all the fighters, who had defeated whom, and the match schedules. By default, I knew them too.

'Mom, do you like John Cena?' he asked me one day.

I made a mental flip-through of the facts about John Cena that I had in my head and decided that yes, I indeed liked him. Here was a wrestler who was not only good looking, but was also a rapper and an actor. But I had never really thought about whether I 'liked' John Cena or not. As far as I was concerned, we occupied different worlds and he didn't matter enough for me to strongly dislike him.

'Hmm. I never really thought about it, but he is okay, I guess,' I told my son.

'Ma, how can you say he is okay? He is *the* best!' The outrage in my son's voice was evident. How could his mother not worship his idol, the same way he did?

'Yeah ma, you should see him fight. He is just awesome,' piped in my six-year-old daughter. She was at that age where she followed everything that her older brother did. Whatever he said was gospel. If he said he liked vegetables with chilli sauce, she would declare that it was her favourite food too. If he said Pokemons were cool, she would agree.

'What do you really like about John Cena?' I asked her.

'Ma, you should see him fight,' she answered.

When my son saw that John Cena's fighting prowess was having no impact on me whatsoever, he decided to go down a different path to make me see light.

'Just think about this – what if John Cena was your husband?' asked my son.

I paused for a second and thought about it.

Then I said, 'What if he was your father? Would you like it?'

My daughter was all ears in this interesting 'adult discussion' between her hero – her older brother, not John Cena – and her other role model, her mother.

It was my son's turn to think.

'Hmm. Maybe I would like it. It would be cool,' my son replied.

'Well, I definitely would not like him to be my husband. Definitely not. Undoubtedly and with great certainty I can say that I would not.'

'And why not? How are you so sure?'

'Can you imagine John Cena helping me in the kitchen? I don't think he would have the time,' I said.

'Ah, you have a point there. That might be something he might not do,' agreed my son.

'And can you imagine me cooking for him? Do you know the amount of food he eats? I'd probably be in the kitchen all the time, rustling up his meals. He would need one meal after the other. After all, he is a body-builder. He needs to eat a tonne of food,' I added.

My daughter now got the hang of it.

'And Ma,' she contributed, her eyes as big as saucers to emphasise the point that she was making, 'John Cena would never have time to help us with homework.'

'Or take you to the park.'

'If he played pretend-wrestling with us, we would be dead!' This little input from my son had me chuckling at the astuteness of the observation.

'He would only have time for his gym, his crunches, his workouts and all that they do,' my daughter added to the discussion.

'So, we don't want John Cena. We will stick to papa,' I concluded.

Both kids laughed and agreed to this.

Meanwhile, my husband who was at work, was blissfully unaware that he had been pitted against one of the best specimens of alpha male on planet earth.

When he came home that evening, the kids told him, 'Papa, you are the best. You know, you are a million times better than John Cena.'

He smiled smugly, looked at me and said, 'Of course. That is why your mother married me, not him.'

All of us laughed at that one.

Round one to the father of my kids.

That night, I thought about families, marriages and about raising children. In an environment where the lines of communication are open, children learn to express themselves. In an autocratic, authoritative environment, everybody's guard is up. When you have open conversations about anything, where you can discuss every thought you have, and nothing is taboo, then you get an insight into even the most difficult issues. This is true for even relationships.

We need to talk. We need to communicate. And we all need to be understood.

There is a deep need in all of us to be loved and accepted for who we truly are.

And yes, it holds good, even if you are John Cena.

A-ha moments

A newspaper article I once read spoke about "A-ha moments" – moments which were eureka moments; when you overcame odds and celebrated victories. They spoke to several people who had many things to share. A fashion designer said that her A-ha moment was when she started practising Nichiren Daishonin's Buddhist philosophy. A socialite said that her A-ha moment was when she became Miss Delhi for the first time. A holistic healer said that her A-ha moment was when she noticed the sun line of a client dipping and she advised some Feng Shui changes which saved her life. (Her client's, not her own!). It was a moment, which they said was an eye-opener for them. They became wiser because of that moment. Their lives became richer. They were not necessarily turning points in their lives, but it stirred something within them. It made them look at situations in a new light, a new perspective.

As for me, I lead a life a little less flamboyant and a little more ordinary. I thought long and hard about my own A-ha moments. Did I have any? As I reflected some more, I realised that I did have them. In fact, I have several.

I had one recently when I realised that I had forgotten to put on the chappals that I usually wear at home (yes, I'm a true Indian,

Hawai chappals would be an apt term for them as every Indian knows) and my son who was seven at that time, forgot to put away his Lego blocks. It was an A-ha moment. To be precise, it was an Aaaaaaaaa-haaaaa moment. Ever tried stepping on Lego blocks with bare feet? I'd strongly recommend that you don't. One can do without such A-ha moments. But if you have had one, they change your life. You learn an important parenting skill, if your children are of a certain age. You learn to wear adequate footwear at all times and be ever-alert.

After the Lego blocks A-ha moment, there was another when I discovered that potato wedges – the variety that needs to go into boiling oil straight from the freezer – can actually explode, sending tiny ripples of oil, zooming out of the frying pan, onto your face. Your face, with its sizzling bits of skin, now begins to resemble a teenager afflicted with acute acne, except that this one does not fade away with Clearasil or other pimple zapping concoctions that promise miracles along with the desirable guy, or a girl – whatever you prefer!

Another defining A-ha moment occurred when the house-help did an AWOL. I ventured forth bravely armed with a bucket and a mop (how hard can it be, after all – and I hate my floors to be dirty) to do the sweeping-mopping. It was truly an Aaaa-aaaaa-haaa moment. Muscles that I didn't know existed even after torturous ab-crunching daily in the gym, made their appearance like guest roles that a movie star plays in his home productions. For the rest of the day, I walked exactly the way Giant Robot used to walk in the live action series that used to be re-run on Doordarshan – the national television channel in India during our school days, when it was in vogue to watch them.

Of course, they are A-ha moments! Where you overcome odds and celebrate victories. What else can you call them? You learn to navigate the treacherous traps of life better, once you have had them. You emerge stronger, wiser and better prepared.

Who says you have to be a socialite or a Miss Delhi to experience these? We can create our very own A-ha moments, especially if you are a bit of a scatterbrain like me, when it comes to running a home.

Good days and bad days

Any parent who has school-going children will aver that life can be divided into good days, bad days and really bad days. I know, as I have lived them and survived to tell the tale.

On a good day, there are more things scattered across my bedroom floor than landmines in a battlefield in World War II. These range from story books, parts of toys, bits of craft material, colouring books, crayons, markers with caps off and caps with markers off. On a bad day, let's just say I have an intense longing to have powers like Moses who parted the sea.

On a good day, I organise a 'Let's-see-who-collects-the-maximum-things-in-one-minute' contest with enthusiastic participation from husband and two kids, the prize being that the winner gets a specially baked treat from me. The husband wins on most good days. He says the prize is irresistible. On a bad day, I organise my vocal chords and yell. Loudly. It always works, the fringe benefit being that since I am grumpy and in a bad mood, I get to sleep by myself in the six-by-six bed. I simply love the fringe benefits.

On a good day, I drag myself out of bed, after hitting the snooze button on the alarm dock at least thrice, trying ineptly to keep my eyes open, light the stove and make coffee… all at the same time. On a bad day, the kids drag me out of bed with rhythmic chants of 'Wake up, Ma – we will be late. Wake up, Ma – it's already eight.'

On a good day, the kids have at least three serious fights in a span of forty-five minutes, before getting ready for school, punctuated liberally with yells of 'Mom, *he* is killing me. Come quick!' to 'Mom, *she* started it. She bit me first. If you don't do something, I'll call the police.' On a bad day, it is the husband and I who fight. We don't yell – but the silent, cold war with hostilities cleverly disguised, gritted teeth, fake sweetness, dripping sarcasm and veiled digs cannot be missed.

On a good day, the tie and the identity card to be worn to school are found after a fifteen-minute search expedition that involves maid, granny and a hassled dad and even more harassed mom, searching frantically in all places, especially inside the washing machine. On a bad day, it is found after a half-hour search and a forced confession extracted from one of the kids that they actually hid the other child's tie, after a fight. On a really bad day, we find it *after* we have filled up a form and paid the fine at school for losing it.

On a good day, I get to read the newspaper at 10:30 am, after everyone has left. On a bad day, I discover that the newspaper has been used to wrap a school project that has to be turned in, and I discover this after I have looked in every possible place that it could be, including under the mattress, just in case the kids hid it there, as revenge for my yelling on a bad day.

On a good day, I always remind myself, there are days which can be worse. On a bad day, I am reminded what Charlene Ann Baumbich said, 'Mama said there'd be days like this – but she didn't say how many!'

I'm thankful for the good days. I'm thankful for the bad days, too. It means that I am well and healthy. I don't have any serious ailments to worry about. I have a happy family and a cosy home. Besides, I can always have a great haircut on a bad day. My hairdresser tells me she styles it best, when it is standing up.

Now my children are all grown up, and the good days and bad days do not exist anymore. There is just the same monotony of long days stretching ahead with no disruptions, no hunt for lost things, no stuff lying on the floor and everything running in clockwork order.

So these days, when people tell me, 'Have a nice day!' I smile and say to myself, 'I think I will.'

Hamsters incorporated

Dealing with loss of any kind is hard. Be it health (sometimes reversible) or a pet (many a time replaceable) or a loved one (never reversible, never replaceable).

One of my friends in the UK had a white mouse as a pet and it was dying. It reminded me of our hamsters, in whose company the children and I had spent many happy hours.

We had never intended to keep hamsters. What I intended to get for my son's birthday was a pair of chicks which we could easily get from a pet store. My house-help was excited as she said she would love to raise them. She wanted me to get females as she was looking forward to the eggs that they would lay later.

So we set out to the pet store, an enthusiastic mother and two excited children. The pet shop owner knew how to charm prospective customers. He introduced us to the hamsters. Then he put one in his pocket and it peeped out so endearingly, with eyes like buttons, resembling Stuart Little. We were completely sold. My son begged and begged for one. I couldn't refuse. It was his birthday after all. And it was indeed easier than keeping a dog or a cat. The chicks were forgotten.

So we came back with two hamsters and a hamster house. My husband, who is not an animal-lover, was aghast. He had not expected it. But now, he had no say in the matter. The house-help was befuddled. She had never seen hamsters before and she asked if they were 'golden rats without tails'.

The children were overjoyed. They fell in love with them and christened them Smart and Cutie. But I was having none of these "modern English names", so I changed their names to Chunnu and Munnu. The names I gave them stuck. Every waking hour that the children were home was spent with Chunnu and Munnu.

Then a problem struck. My father-in-law was visiting us for a few days. He does not approve of pets at all, and he thinks they cause health hazards. Of all the things, if he saw hamsters, we were certain we would have to listen to many hours of lecture on 'The danger of keeping pets and what harm they can cause'.

I warned the children that if their grandfather came to know of the new pets, they would have to go right back to the store. Now they were accomplices in the crime. My husband too was roped in. He didn't want to listen to the lectures as well.

My father-in-law arrived the next day. All of us were now players in this 'hide-the-hamsters' game. We kept the hamsters in their cage, in my son's room, and kept the door locked. The kids were on high alert. Whenever their grandfather tried to enter the room, one of them would distract him and take him elsewhere.

We managed to keep him out of that room, but we had several close calls.

Like the time the hamsters let themselves out of the cage. They are very intelligent beings and great escape artistes. It is very difficult to find hamsters once they escape, as they are tiny and agile. We were also very worried, that in case my father-in-law woke up at night and saw them, he would probably kill them, mistaking them for rats.

After a few breathless moments, we did manage to find both of them, happily hiding inside an old shoe that had been shoved under the cupboard. We later made elaborate tunnels for them with cardboard, and they loved climbing and going around in the tunnels.

Chunnu-Munnu were Syrian golden hamsters. It was great fun to watch how they interacted with each other. They had petty fights with each other, just like humans. Munnu (the female) would then sulk, and Chunnu would try to make peace, by offering her either a twig, or sunflower seeds or nuts. She would then reluctantly agree to accept it. (I am sure secretly, she wanted to just run to him, but hey, she should not give in so easily, right? Make the guy beg a little.) And in no time they would be 'in action'. Their efforts produced a few lovely babies, some of which Munnu ate. I was horrified to learn that hamsters do eat their young ones sometimes.

One of the babies survived. Again the children came up with some fancy name. But I very imaginatively called it 'Chunnu-munnu-baby'. Somehow no other name seemed apt.

The average lifespan of the hamster is two years. Chunnu and Munnu, both died, one after the other. I wish I could tell you that Munnu died of a broken heart. Who knows, but scientists and rational thinkers would just attribute it to things like lifespan, and the natural ageing process.

We had many good times with Chunnu-munnu-baby. We used to watch his antics with delight. He, like his parents, learnt to let himself out of the cage. He could identify me and my son. My daughter was a bit reluctant to handle him, but loved petting him.

My husband too grew fond of him. But he would only watch him. He was too terrified to touch him or hold him.

One of my closest friends came over to stay with us. Her children too fell in love with Chunnu-munnu-baby. But my friend, like my husband, stayed far away.

It was comical for us to hear how my husband perfected the art of feeding them when the kids and I went to visit my mom for a few days. He was petrified of opening their cage. So he perfected the fine art of dropping sunflower seeds into their bowl through the gap at the top of the cage, his hand positioned very scientifically at a ninety-degree angle, which would ensure that they all fell right into the bowl.

The hamster was alive and happy when we came back and my husband's aim had been perfected. If there was a feeding-hamster-without-opening-cage-contest, he would have won it! I guess some people are comfortable with animals and some just are not.

There was always a bunch of kids over at my place those days, as they were all fascinated by the hamster.

For all the trouble that losing the hamsters involved, I cherish the happy memories that we had with Chunnu-munnu-baby. Not to mention, it was an enriching experience and a learning process filled with joy for the kids.

Life in all forms is to be revered and if you manage to do that, you manage to see the magic in it.

Some facts about hamsters
- Hamsters are one of the easiest pets to keep, especially if you live in an apartment. They can be obtained from any reputed pet shop. They are nocturnal creatures. They have cheek pouches that they use to store food. They later bring the food out and add it to a stock that they keep, just like squirrels do.
- They don't need to be vaccinated and they do not spread any disease. On the contrary, they can catch a cold from you! Therefore, it is you who have to be careful about your own hygiene lest the hamster catches an infection from you. The average lifespan of the hamster is about two years and many parents buy a hamster as a pet to teach their children about the joy of caring for another being, as also dealing with death and loss.

Mama said it

Has it ever happened to you that when someone makes a slightly disparaging remark, you don't know what to say right then? Hours later when you are thinking about it, a smart repartee strikes you and then you wish that you had thought of it at that point of time. It has happened to me sometimes. I think of a clever line, but only hours later.

Some people are blessed with quick wit and some train themselves. I don't know which category my mother falls into, but it sure is hard to escape her words that are like a shower of bullets from a machine gun, leaving you with multiple holes in your ego, not knowing what to say or do.

Conversations with her always bring me back to earth with a thud. Sometimes the thud is so softly cushioned that I don't even realise that I have *thud-ed* until the pain spreads slowly. It is like brilliant crimson of the sunrise, filling up a portion of the drab blue sky.

She has a great sense of humour and an arsenal of ready wit, cleverly clothed in a cloak of sarcasm that unless you are sharp, you don't even realise how her veiled dig just deflated your puffed-up ego as gently as air being let out from one of those travel air pillows.

If you are not used to her, you will most definitely gape with open mouth, not knowing what to say. But if you have grown up with her, you get used to her ways. You become amusing, clever, witty, sarcastic and at the same time, 'aggressive in a gentle way'. There is no other way to describe it, although I am aware it is an oxymoron.

My memories of my mother's clever retorts are many, but one that I remember in vivid detail is this one. There was a pesky guy, a distant relative, who used to keep dropping in, uninvited. There was no getting away from those unexpected visits, and we just learnt to put up with it. They would usually be just before meal times and we would be forced to offer him a meal as we couldn't possibly eat without asking him to join us.

I could sense that my mother did not like him much. He would make himself very comfortable at a time that was convenient to *him*. Then he would speak about what he did, and where he went and how great he was. He would go on and on. When he ran out of breath or out of topics, he would keep inviting us over to his home. We never went.

After several invitations that never resulted in a visit to his home, he said to my mother in mock frustration, 'If the person does not go to the well to drink water, the well has to come to the person.' (He was loosely translating a Hindi proverb.)

'Oh, that really depends on whether the person is thirsty or not,' retorted my mom instantly. It struck home and his unwelcome visits stopped after that. I remember my dad laughing hard over this.

Another time, we were having a surly elderly relative visiting us. My mother, in the true tradition of Indian hospitality, had slaved in the kitchen for hours and prepared a delicious, four-course meal, with many accompaniments. This gentleman enjoyed the scrumptious meal. He took several large helpings but did not utter a word of appreciation or thanks. He then looked at my brother and me and made a snide comment that we looked like a pair of skeletons. He turned to my mother and asked her if she wasn't feeding us enough.

With an absolutely straight face, my mother replied, 'Feed them? Of course, not! On most days I starve them. But when we have *slightly* gluttonous people over, I let them eat. But only a teeny weenie bit, just in case the food falls short.' She smiled sweetly.

He did not expect it and I could see the colour draining from his face. He squirmed embarrassed, as the point had hit home.

My mother does not hesitate to say whatever is on her mind. She is forthright and frank. She has a way of putting it, exactly like it is. It is hard to get the better of her. She also has a comic sense of narrating events and, telephone conversations with her are always laugh sessions.

When she was visiting me recently, I took her for a master health check-up to the hospital. We had to fill up the hospital forms and I was doing it for her.

There was a column for "Father's/Husband's name".

I found it meaningless to fill that in as neither her husband nor her father were even alive. How did it matter?

I didn't tell her anything though. The pain of losing my dad still opens up raw wounds inside me.

'What should I write? Father's name or husband's name?' I asked her.

'Strike that out, write daughter's name and put your name there,' said my mom, very matter of fact.

And with that statement, in her quiet unassuming straight-forward way, she struck down the centuries of the subtle, powerful patriarchal system that our great India is steeped in.

She is an amazing person, my mom.

And my strength too.

The Gnome syndrome

There's a gnome in my house. (And no, I am not referring to my husband.) I have never seen him but I know he exists. He visits only when I am sleeping or when I have stepped out.

At times, he is mean. He leaves the computer on for hours at end. He leaves the hot water geyser switched on in the bathroom, for almost the whole day, even when it is not needed. He is not a fan of energy conservation or cutting electricity bills. He simply doesn't care.

A favourite activity of his is dropping crumbs of food on the carpet. This is usually done when I have stepped out of the house with strict instructions to those at home that nothing that can be chewed and consumed should be brought within three square feet of the outward edges of the carpet. The instructions as well as the measurements are completely ignored.

Another favourite activity of his is "hide the slipper". He quietly hides one slipper of mine and I have to hunt for hours before I find it. He usually does that after I have ticked off one of the kids for something they did or didn't do – whatever is applicable. I suspect he is fond of kids. He has a particular affinity for the sketch pens and markers that the children use. He always leaves the caps off so

21

that they dry up and become useless. He also messes up perfectly tidy cupboards – I think he likes to create work for me.

He leaves toothpaste tubes with the caps off, in the bathroom. He wets the soap and leaves it outside the soap container. He leaves wet towels on the bed. If the bed is made he will be sure to pull a corner of the sheet and yank out a pillow or two so that it looks unmade.

If there is a single tomato remaining in the refrigerator, he always eats it, so that the next day when I am making *baingan bhartha* and am desperately looking for the tomato (after roasting the brinjal and chopping the onion), I discover that it is not there.

If footwear is kept inside the shoe-rack where it is supposed to be, you can be sure he will take them out and deliberately leave them lying exactly where you trip over them as soon as you enter the house. He does that with skateboards too – and skateboards are so much more dangerous than footwear. Now I have learnt not to complain much as long as he sticks to footwear.

Sometimes he even answers my mobile phone when it rings if I am not around – and it is maddening. And no, I cannot ask him who called because he always evades me.

He leaves story books where they shouldn't be. But I don't mind that so much because I love to read and everywhere I turn in my house there is a book.

These days he is more active than ever.

All the traps that I have set to catch him have failed miserably. He always outsmarts me – always. Never have I managed to win.

I don't know what he looks like but I do know his name. It is "I-didn't-do-it-Mommy".

Preeti's laws of parenting

After nearly two decades of being a parent, there is a certain wisdom one gains. If you have children of your own, I am certain you will relate to these laws. If you don't have children, but you have been a child at some point in time, then you will relate to this too – especially as certain points here can be equally applicable if you just replace 'school' with 'office'. I condense my findings into:

Preeti's laws of parenting (with due respect to Murphy's laws):

1. No matter how organised you think you are on a Sunday evening to face the Monday morning rush, you are never organised enough.
2. Clean socks always choose Monday mornings to vanish.
3. If clean socks are found, you get mismatched pairs. I am convinced it is a conspiracy hatched by the Secret Society of Single Socks.
4. Precisely a day after you have got rid of the single socks which you had saved for ages just in case its partner was found, its partner turns up in all its splendour, perfect and clean. ('Out, out you damned socks!' I have learnt that the best way is to be merciless and throw them out, no matter how good they look.)

5. School t-shirts vanish mysteriously. Sometimes they turn up at sports lockers in schools. Sometimes they turn up in the chest of drawers where the socks are supposed to be. Sometimes they are found stuffed under the bed. On some occasions they will even be found inside the car. How they travel there will always remain a mystery.

6. The projects to be handed in, homework to be done and charts to be submitted are announced exactly on the last day that it has to be handed in and always when there is only half an hour left for school to start. Gestapo questioning the previous day is always met with strong denial that nothing is due and nothing is pending.

7. School shoes go wandering all around the house. They have a designated place, but they also have a tendency to roam. The latter usually overcomes the former.

8. Parent-teacher meetings where they specify that you cannot bring the younger sibling(s) are always held when the spouse is travelling. If spouse is in town, then they are held on days where the spouse has a very important meeting that cannot be missed.

9. If you have two children, you can be sure they will have diametrically opposite tastes in food. If one likes rice-dal-sabji, the other won't touch it even with a bargepole and would prefer garlic baguettes and hash browns which the first would claim to be allergic to.

10. Fights and decibel levels get magnified a thousand fold when you're single parenting, when spouse is travelling. Sometimes they also get magnified at the mere prospect of single parenting. If there is nothing to complain about, children will always find a way. 'Maaa – he is breathing my air!' (…and I am tearing out my hair!)

11. Sometimes going out for a walk and walking really fast solves all problems, provided the 'stomping out in anger' bit is staged well enough. It works only if they realise you have gone. So staying out of sight for at least an hour is recommended. It can get boring to be on your own, so it is highly recommended that you carry your purse, iPod and mobile before stomping out.

12. No matter what you do or do not do, your children will *always* give you another chance! So will your spouse.

13. All the above will still continue, even when they are teens and are perfectly capable of handling their own stuff. Walking still holds good, especially when you are ready to explode.

Despite all the above laws, you will always find a way to solve any problem – real or imaginary.

You will also feel completely on top of the world when their arms go around you, giving you the tightest hug ever and telling you that you are the 'bestest' parent in the whole universe.

How to get teens to
clean their rooms

'Mom, now that I have finished my studies, can I have the iPad
that you put away?'

'I'll give it to you just now.'

15 minutes later.

'Mom, can I have the iPad?'

'Yes. Wait.'

10 minutes later.

'Mom, you said I could have the iPad. Can you at least tell me
where you hid it?'

'I will give it to you.'

12 minutes later.

'Mom, please can I have the iPad?'

'Yes. I will. Will do it in a bit.'

10 minutes later.

'*Mom* – are you even listening to me? Or are you in zombie
mode?'

'Shhh… I am reading. Let me finish this.'

5 minutes later.

'Mom – are you done? iPad please?'

'I am not yet done. 5 minutes. I promise.'

5 minutes later.

'Mom– 5 minutes are up.'

'Oh, is it? Just coming.'

'Mom! I want the iPad. *Please!'*

'Now you know exactly how I feel when I ask you to clean your room.'

'Aaaaargh!!'

Fifteen minutes later, we have the cleanest room in the world, a contented mother and a slightly surly-but-happy teen, each absorbed in doing what they love best, be it reading or fiddling on the iPad.

The perfect pet

When we moved to the UK, my children adjusted to the new country very quickly. They loved it, and took to it like ducks to water. Large parks, great schools, lovely neighbourhood, new friends, and to top it all – the children also got a new pet.

The pet was an outstanding and unique one. Most parents would agree that after the initial enthusiasm for a new pet wanes, the chores connected with pet care will invariably become the duty of the parents. But with this pet, we had absolutely no such problems. It was intelligent, smart and very well-trained. It groomed itself and really needed almost no looking after. It never came in with dirty paws and neither did it shed hair. It was toilet-trained and most amazingly, it used the loo; and can you believe this – even knew how to use the flush! And no, I am not kidding. Can you imagine having a pet and no chores like cleaning up afterwards? This pet was so wonderful that it even fed itself. The children were in love with it and completely adored it. The sad part was that they remembered it mostly only when they had no friends to play with. Otherwise it was neglected and left to amuse itself. But it never complained. It faithfully greeted them every single day when they returned from school and oh, the love it showered on them! It was such a pleasure to see their faces lighting up with joy when they saw it. Another superb thing was that this pet would finish leftovers in a jiffy. The children simply left their soggy cornflakes or squished-up Chocos, or even milk half drunk, and they did not even have to offer it to the pet. They would leave these half-finished meals and go to school or to play, depending on the time of the day, and when they came back, their meal would have been polished off and their plate, clean. It saved them from getting a yelling from their dad for not finishing their meal so many times.

This pet was so intuitive, it just knew what exactly had to be done.

At night, when they had nightmares, all they had to do was call out to it by name and say, 'I am feeling scared.' In a trice, it would be beside them, comforting them so that they went to sleep peacefully after that.

If I told you that this pet even knew how to pick up wet towels from the floor, you would probably think I am exaggerating – but it is true. It was so intelligent and clever, I was always amazed by it. Not only did it pick up wet towels that the children had dropped to the floor after their baths, but it even made their beds and put away their toys. It was that well-trained.

Can you guess what kind of a pet this was? Was it a dog? Was it a monkey? Was it a trained parakeet? What could it have possibly been?

It was a unique thing – a combination of all the above. It still does all these things up to this day and it responds when they call it 'Mommy.'

What your mother really wants

The first message I got on Mother's Day was from my own mother. 'Happy Mother's Day' she had texted. I called her up and wished her the same.

Much is made of Mother's Day. Spas declare a 'bring-your-mom-at-a-fifty-percent-discount' offer. Opticians offer incentives for your mother's spectacles. Hospitals offer a free check-up. Card shops display the gifts you can get for your mother, apart from the cloyingly sentimental cards cleverly written to tug at your heart-strings and make you go *aww*.

But has anyone bothered to ask their mothers what they would like from their children?

Here are three letters written from the point of view of mothers of children in three age groups:

0–12 years: Apple-of-my-eye
13–21 years: My Young Star
21 and above: The adult child

Dearest Apple-of-my-eye,

Thank you so much for the lovely card you sat up making for me. It is beautiful. Thank you too for the breakfast in bed that you made with your dad. The mess that you left in the kitchen, the aftermaths of the above-mentioned breakfast, for me to clear up is okay. It is after all a small thing compared to the grand gesture. Thank God you don't do it every day. Okay – don't sulk. I was only kidding. I appreciate it. Really, I do.

All I ask from you this Mother's Day is a promise. A promise to put in your best effort in all that you do. It is going to be hard. After all, who does not like an easy path? But I want you to make me a promise that you will go the extra mile. If your teacher has said that a certain lesson will be done in the next class, make an effort and read that lesson beforehand. Make notes of the concepts you did not understand, and want better clarity on. Read up things related to your topic. Do not just do your homework; but also do a little more. Study hard.

Take part in all the activities that you can, in school. Be enthusiastic. It does not matter if you do not qualify. The important thing is to have tried.

Be nice to people you meet. Be polite. But do not let anyone push you around. Stand up for what you believe in.

I am always with you, every step of the way.

Lots of love,
Mom

Dearest Young Star,

How quickly you have grown! I sometimes just cannot believe that just the other day, you were a baby, needing me for everything. Now, sometimes, it is me who needs you.

You question me a lot on all that I say. And it leaves me exasperated at times, but you know what – I secretly like it. I know you have your own logic, your own way of looking at things, your own ideas. I am proud of that. It shows you are growing – becoming a person in your own right, ready to take on all that the world throws at you.

The choices before you may be puzzling at times. You may not have figured out whether you want to go in for science or an education in liberal arts or any of the many such options. You may be constantly asked, 'So, what career have you decided on?' and you may have no clue. You know what, it is okay. It will come to you. Give it time, and see what you are naturally drawn to. Do not go by peer pressure and never do something just because that's what all your friends are doing. (Yes, the famous phrase which all parents use – just because all your friends jump off a bridge, will you – still holds wisdom.)

I know you just can't wait to be an adult. But enjoy this phase. It will be gone before you realise it.

And yes – please clean your room, make your bed, take your laundry for wash, and please be polite. That's all I ask of you, this Mother's Day.

Lots of love,
Mom

Dear Adult Child,

Please call me at least twice a week. Speak to me. Tell me about your work. I may not understand all that you do, but I like listening to you.

That is all I ask of you, this Mother's Day.

I miss you, you know.

Lots of love,
Mom

LIFE, LOVE AND LAUGHTER

"Life is worth living as long as there's a laugh in it."

– L.M. Montgomery

The gift of laughter

For a relationship to sustain, one thing that is just as important as love, is laughter. Laughter makes it fun. Laughter is the shortest distance between two hearts and laughter is a gift that you find in the most unexpected places. It surprises you like an unexpected shower on a hot summer afternoon. And before you realise it, it is gone, leaving you with sweet memories that sometimes last a lifetime. Laughter is something I seek out consciously, and strangely, I have discovered that when you seek it, you do find it. Okay I confess – if I don't find it, I orchestrate by planning and plotting to make it happen. *Tee-he. Ha-ha!*

The women in my family have an innate ability to laugh at just about anything. I remember how my grandmother used to laugh a lot. You just had to tell her something remotely funny and she would chuckle and guffaw and soon we would all join in. Laughter, like yawns, is infectious.

My mother too has inherited this trait and she has a terrific sense of humour, often childlike and extremely funny. You clutch your sides laughing at something she said or something she did.

When we were children, one of her favourite activities was to startle one of us with a loud bang made by bursting a brown paper bag or a plastic cover. She would blow air into it and twist the ends so that it looked like a balloon. And then when we were least expecting it, she would creep up quietly behind us and burst it.

My brother and I learnt quickly to anticipate it. It would usually be on the day we bought pure peaberry coffee powder that came in a brown bag, which was a size ideal for filling with air and bursting. The temptation was irresistible for her.

When we became smarter and learnt to avoid her little bang-expedition, she found a new victim – my dad. No matter how many times she did it, my poor dad got caught unawares most of the time. He would be intently reading the newspaper, or studying the stock market data in a magazine, when my mom would creep up behind him, with my brother and me suppressing giggles in the background. She would then burst the paper cover. BANG! The explosion was deafening and dad would be so startled that he would drop the paper or magazine. And then when he had recovered, he would join in the delighted, mad and absolutely crazy laughter. He was always a sport.

My children soon learnt what a fun activity it actually is. Many years back, my son came back from school with a sheepish look saying that he had been punished in class but he had enjoyed it so much that he wouldn't mind getting punished again for doing it. When asked what he had done – yes, you guessed it – in the middle of Math class, he had burst a paper bag, nearly sending the teacher rocketing into space, he added gleefully. I suppressed my urge to laugh and told him sternly that he should respect the teacher and not ever repeat it again. With that I dusted my hands off the parenting duty. As soon as he was out of earshot, I called my mom, narrated it to her and we both burst into delighted chuckles of secret approval.

I don't burst paper bags like my mom did. (Okay, I admit, I have done it a couple of times, but *only* a couple.) But the one thing that

I love to do is hide behind the door when someone is entering the room and then shout, "BOOOO", jumping out suddenly. I am sure many of you must have done it too at some point in your lives. It is hilarious to see the look of surprise on the face of the person and then watch it changing to shocked relief. Usually the person joins in the laughter. I have startled my friends and cousins many times like this and then gone into paroxysms of laughter at this very childish prank.

One evening, when I saw my husband's car pulling up into the driveway, on an impulse I decided that it was the perfect opportunity to play this trick on him, especially as he follows the unvarying routine of never ringing the doorbell. Instead, he lets himself in with his key. Then he enters the house and calls out for me.

That day, when I saw his car pulling up, I swiftly hid behind the door so that the moment he put his key in, opened the door and entered, I would pounce out – like a panther, I thought wickedly – and shout, "GRRRRR" or "Bowwww" or "Booooo" or whatever noise struck me as most appropriate at that point. I imagined striking terror in his heart with my decibel level. Heart racing, I positioned myself, listening carefully for his footsteps and for the click of the key in the door. The moment he stepped in, with perfect timing, I jumped out like a Jack-in-the-box and let out a ear-shattering yell –'BHHHHHOOOOOOW!' The person who jumped into the air wasn't my husband (he was used to my crazy ways, after all) but the very startled insurance salesman who had come home with my husband so that they could go over a policy that my husband was interested in.

He must have got the fright of his life, poor guy, at this crazy, mad woman who his potential client was married to. I think it was only his eagerness to sell the policy that prevented him from throwing his hands up in the air and running out screaming in terror. My husband was not amused. He tried to pretend nothing **had** happened.

But me? I really could not control my laughter. I ran into the **kitchen**, out of sight of both of them and collapsed laughing on the floor.

Like I was telling you, laughter springs up on you when you least expect it or maybe it is because I orchestrate it with precise (okay, sometimes impulsive) planning.

But hey – what's life and relationships without laughter?

The scooter Romeo

Anyone who has children under the age of five, will tell you what a long process it is, if you have to travel with them in the car, even for a short distance. There are a hundred things like toys, diapers, changing mat, wet wipes, baby powder, lotion, a drink, a snack, sippys, favourite blanket, books, etc., that you have to load into the car apart from the car seat. And if one of the children is just a baby, then the work automatically triples.

When my daughter was a three-month-old baby, and my son was about three-and-a-half years old, I had a very sweet girl called Mary who lived with me for a while, to help me look after the children. My husband used to travel a lot those days, and Mary was a life-saver.

If we ever wanted to go out, the operation of loading the car was a fifteen-minute process, which had to be executed in precise order, like a military operation. The drill was that we would load the car in the following order:

1. My daughter's Moses basket. She was too small to be held up for long periods of time and was most comfortable travelling this way.

2. My daughter's bag that contained her diapers, baby food, clean towels, warm water in a thermos flask and a hundred and fifty other things that three-month-old babies need.

3. A large soft pillow to rock my daughter to sleep – she had a favourite one. If the pillow ever went missing, the screams she would let out would be louder than the ones you would hear in the Gestapo torture department.

4. My son's toy bag consisting of toy bulldozers, fire engines, dinky cars and Lego models that he had made. He would insist on carrying them around wherever we went. I have no idea why. You can never reason with a three-and-a-half-year-old. When they say they want something, they want it. If you don't give it to them, they torture you with their bawls. So it's easier to carry whatever they want.

5. A clean blanket to cover the car seat in case any of the children throw up; tissues, hand wipes, nose wipes, bum wipes and every other wipe that has ever been manufactured.

6. My daughter.

7. My son.

8. Mary, who would keep an eye on my daughter when she fell asleep in the Moses basket.

9. And finally, finally… me, to drive the car.

It was a great task and I considered it an accomplishment to get everything and everybody in that order respectively, into the car. And this drill was *after* we all got ready. Getting each child and ourselves ready was another operation altogether.

Mary would usually sit in the rear seat with both the children and I would be the chauffer, driving the car. I couldn't put my three-and-a-half-year-old son in the front. Once we reached our destination, the unloading process would start in the reverse order.

We had done this so many times that we had perfected it, down to the last detail.

On one such expedition I was feeling very pleased with myself because I had just got a new pair of sunglasses. I thought I looked stylish and sophisticated. As we drove on, I noticed some roadside Romeos whistling at me. One of them waved, but I ignored him.

'Idiots, have they never seen a woman in cool sunglasses?' I muttered under my breath as I looked right through them as I set forth on my mission, with two children and Mary.

Within a few seconds I noticed some more guys staring, waving and whistling. I had no idea what to make of it. Then to my horror, I saw a guy in the rear view mirror, speeding up on a scooter behind me and waving. I transformed into a ferocious lioness protecting her cubs. The only weapon that the lioness had in this case being the accelerator pedal in the car. I stepped on it, secretly pleased that I had a valid reason to put my finely honed driving skills garnered over the years, to good use. Hah! I always knew my driving skills would come in handy one day, to protect my babies from the dangerous scooter Romeos on the roads.

We sped and swerved and I felt like Sean Boswell in *Fast and the Furious*, with the voice inside me screaming, 'If you ain't outta control, you ain't in control.' Mary was hanging on for dear life and my three-and-a-half-year-old son was clapping his hands in manic glee shouting, 'Mummy race! Go, mummy go.'

Mummy went but what mummy did not foresee was the darned traffic light and so mummy had to slow down. The Romeo-on-the-scooter now caught up with me. I could see him in the rear view mirror. 'Please change traffic light, please change to green,' I prayed. But it did not. I took a quick look again. He was pulling up right beside my car. I was a bit frightened now. He was waving something white at me like a truce flag and was mouthing what

I thought were the words, 'Madame — *eshtop!*' He then pulled up beside me and said, 'Madame — *aapka pillow, yeh gaadi ke upaar tha aur ghir gaya.*' (Madame, your pillow. It was on top of the car and it fell down.)

I looked at Mary and she very sheepishly said, '*Ayyo —akka, naan car mele vechen akka — marundu poyitten.*' (I had kept it on the hood of the car. I forgot to take it when I got in.)

That meant I had been speeding like Jhansi *ki* Rani with the pillow fluttering on top of my car. God! The embarrassment and the bashfulness I felt when I realised it! I did manage to thank him, however. The Romeo-on-the-scooter had suddenly turned into Nicholas Cage in *Ghost Rider,* minus the hell-blazing, of course. I flashed him what he must have thought was a million watt smile, but what I knew was a very embarrassed, oh-no-how-could-I smile.

Thank God I was wearing sun glasses. They manage to make you look very cool, even when you're squirming on the inside.

Bumpity-bump

Twice in my life, I have been confined to the bed with strict orders from the doctor to not leave the supine position except for essentials. It was for both my pregnancies. Both times the doctors felt that the baby might not gain enough weight as I was too active; and so confined me to bed for almost ten weeks. I am conscientious when it comes to health, especially my children's health. I followed the doctor's instructions like a good girl and did not move from the bed at all.

For my first pregnancy, I was in Kerala, staying with my parents, as my husband had a job that involved very hectic travel abroad. Those were the days when there were no smartphones and no internet. As soon as the doctor announced that I had to be confined to bed, I insisted that my folks first take me to the library so I could borrow my full quota of ten books, which would last me at least two weeks. After that, when I went for my routine check-up, I would replenish my stock – I had already planned out the strategy for surviving the dreaded 'bed-rest' which is torture of the worst kind, as I am a person who just cannot sit still. My parents, like all parents, wanted me to go home, close my eyes and lie on the bed and rest.

I protested with every pregnant bone in my body. The doctor had told me to rest only physically – not my mind. I'd be unhappy if I had to lie down and do nothing – and shouldn't a pregnant woman be kept happy? Else won't it affect the temperament of the baby? Of course, that last argument clinched the deal. Dad drove me to the library and a worried mom watched as I climbed up the narrow stairs leading to the library, which was housed on the first floor of an ancient building. She asked if she should come with me. I pooh-poohed her suggestion and smiled benignly at her, in what I hoped was an assuring manner. I climbed up confidently while they waited in the car, as there was no parking space available. The stairs were tougher than I thought. But since I had thrown such a tantrum to be taken to the library, there was no way I was admitting defeat. So I mustered up my strength and managed to reach the top, huffing and puffing, like the wolf in the *Three Little Pigs* story, pushing a seven-month pregnant, bulging belly up along with me.

I stumbled into the library with a thin film of sweat covering my forehead. My palms were clammy. Everything in my line of vision was fading. Then I promptly fainted over the librarian's desk. Fortunately, I realised what was happening and I had the presence of mind to sit on a little wooden stool which I spotted in the nick of time, just before I collapsed.

The poor man, a very quiet, nerdy guy like most librarians are, must have jumped out of his skin to see a woman collapse like a bowling pin, that too one who was obviously very pregnant. When I came to consciousness, I saw my dad, my mom, and the very pale-faced librarian peering at me through his glasses. The look of horror, shock and relief on his face, all at the same time, reminded me of someone who had finally managed to take a dump after being constipated. I burst out laughing. You can imagine the reaction of my parents. For added amusement, you can also imagine the reaction of the librarian.

It helps to have an internal switch to turn on, when you do not want to hear something. When I yell at my kids after reaching my wits' end because they have not cleaned their room despite the umpteenth reminder; or have not done their homework or any such task, they say they switch it on, so then, they do not have to hear anything I am saying. They must have inherited this switch from me, because that day in the library, that is what I did too. I turned on my switch and when my parents finished saying whatever they had been saying, I asked calmly if I could borrow my books.

You bet I got my way. I am very persistent. The librarian more than willingly agreed. I am certain he did not want to see my face again and must have been haunted by the nightmare of several pregnant women collapsing on his desk.

I went home with twenty books that day. Now, each time I visit Kerala and pass that library, my mother asks me, 'Do you want to borrow books?' and we chuckle.

A gift for you

Have you ever wondered what to gift your girlfriend or significant other? Or have you been thrown into a tizzy thinking about what to give that 'I-think-it-is-a-crush-but-I am-not-so-sure' kind of a friend? Or have you spent ages trying to decide what to gift your best friend who has everything? If you have, welcome to the club. You are not alone.

Picking the perfect gift is not easy. Not only do you have to know the other person well, but you should also be willing to go the extra mile to pick out that perfect gift. There are several online options, but unless one is prepared to look very hard, it runs the risk of degenerating into something tacky or worse, thoughtless.

One of the ways we express our love for that special person is through gifts. It isn't very different in the animal kingdom. Throughout the animal kingdom, the males of the species have always wooed the females. Mating rituals in the animal kingdom are fascinating. A single male grasshopper has more than 400 songs in his repertoire. I think that's enough to give Elvis Presley and Himesh Reshammiya put together, a complex of being woefully inadequate! Blue whales produce low frequency repetitive booming calls to attract females and ward off other males. The praying mantis is known for a strange mating ritual. The females behead and devour their partners, before, during or after mating. Males try to avoid being eaten through a combination of caution and speed.

Some male insects like the scorpion fly, gift the females tiny packets containing food. At times these packets are empty. They just serve as a clever distraction. While the female tries to open the gift, the male proceeds to mate with her. The rogue – how clever is that?!

I am reminded of my college days and something that happened to my friend Maya. We were in college and I was visiting her at her hostel at that time. Staying in a hostel gives you all kinds of opportunities to be away from the prying eyes of parents. Passing off a boyfriend as a cousin or a family member is as easy as downing a tequila shot. It is intimidating only the first time. After that, the high you get hooks you.

Her boyfriend turned up one morning and gifted her forty cute little teddy bears. Forty! She just couldn't believe it. He had never given her any gift before and this was overwhelming. He had brought them all in a box and left it for her that morning. He had to leave for an important meeting that morning. He was older and had a job in a software company, while we were in our final year of college. He had left a note saying he would visit in the evening.

Maya was delighted. Soft toys always melt women, no matter what their age – and forty of them in a box were unbelievable. All of us gathered around her, admiring the cute little bears. Some of us asked her for one, and Maya being the generous soul that she is, began distributing them to whoever was in her good books at that point of time and whoever pleaded hard enough. Soon she was left with about eleven and she was content with that. After all, what will you do with forty identical bears that vary a little only in colour?

Her boyfriend came in the evening as promised. Maya was beaming. He revelled in the warmth.

'So, did you like them? And did your friends like them?' he asked.

'How did you know that I would give them to my friends?'

'Oh, I know you women,' he replied with a wave of the hand.

She smiled contentedly. They enjoyed the silence that only two people comfortable with each other can. She put her head on his shoulder.

Then he said, 'So, where is the money?'

'What money?' she asked

'The money for the teddy bears,' he said. 'I had left them with you for selling them to your friends. I knew your friends would like them. A friend of mine has started a new gift store.'

Both of us did not know what to say to that. We looked hard to see if he was joking.

He wasn't.

You can imagine what must have happened after that.

A tale of two seahorses

Every Saturday, my column *Sex and the City* appears in the *Financial Chronicle*. (It is now called *Slice of Life*.) To write this column, I research quite a bit, and today, I discovered a lot about seahorses. I was amused to discover that in seahorses, it is the males who carry the babies. The females deposit their eggs in the male's pouch and he carries them till they are ready to hatch.

After I wrote my column, I sat back and imagined a scenario between two seahorses meeting at a bar, and decided to write a dialogue between them, just for fun and to amuse myself.

Here's what I imagined it would be like:

Deep down in the Pacific Ocean, between the coral reefs, two seahorses meet at the sea-weed bar. She is nursing a blue-algae margarita while he swims up to her. She looks at him and looks away, pretending to be disinterested. She checks him out through the corner of her eye though. He notices and gets closer.

'Wanna come back to my cave? Yay or neigh?' he says.

How audacious, she thinks. And what is with the accent, he is probably American. Either that, or he works at a call-centre. She doesn't instantly refuse though. She arches up her spine and sits up a bit more straight on the coral reef bar-stool.

'Excuse me! I have heard far better lines than those.'

But he is not one to be deterred easily.

'I have a nice tight pouch. And I don't charge too much,' he tries again.

'*Charge?* I am not in the market for pouches. Pouches don't interest me much. Seen too many.'

Her reply is a bit too quick.

'Ok, let's go dancing then? You have a nice tail. I was checking it out when you swam in.'

That makes her smile.

'What kind of dance do you do?'

'The horse trot. It's like the fox trot, but for seahorses. I'll teach you. If you're lucky, you may even get to see my pouch later.'

She can't believe how presumptuous he is.

'I work in the International Academy of Horse Dancing. I would teach *you*. But I don't think you can afford me, mister. And I don't wanna see no pouches.'

'So dance just to dance? I want to practice our mating ritual!'

'Umm… nah, not interested. I came here to unwind. Dancing is work for me.'

Ms Seahorse starts checking out other horses at the algae bar.

'What's your favourite sex position?'

'Why would I want to tell you that?'

Mr Seahorse downs his seventh shot.

·'I like horsie style… It's like doggie style, but for us.'

Ms Seahorse gets up and bolts. And looks at the bouncer (an orca whale) and gestures to him with her eyes.

Bouncer steps in.

She swims for her life, swishing her cute tail furiously, getting away as fast as she can.

Mr Seahorse is bewildered. He asks his male friends why he can't get any tail. The last I heard, he was still asking.

Sly Stallone does not open so easily

Have you ever had a laughter attack? Laughed like a lunatic for absolutely no reason? And then, when you are in that mode, everything, every single little thing which is so ordinary seems really funny and you just can't stop laughing. It is a bit like being drunk, except that you are completely sober and in your senses, but your rib has gone into auto-tickling mode, just like a computer that has hung. You convulse helplessly with laughter, tears streaming down your face, clutching your sides and still laughing, even though your tummy hurts.

A friend of mine and I have got into this mode a couple of times. She lived in the apartment next to mine on the sixth floor. Hours after our kids and husbands left for school and work, we would stand on our respective balconies which were adjacent to each other's, talking over a leisurely cup of tea. Our apartment complex was located behind a group of posh office buildings that housed many software giants and multinationals. So it always had a crowd of young office-goers hanging around, taking a break. My friend would pick the best looking guys of the lot, point two out and tell me, 'He is yours and that one there is mine.' I would look

51

at who she picked out and we would giggle like silly school girls, far from the supposedly responsible mothers of two that we were.

She rang my bell frantically one afternoon. The cooking gas cylinder in her house had just got over. If you have lived in India, you'll know what a big disaster this is. Most places in India use LPG cylinders and have not yet switched to piped gas. You would also probably know that sometimes it can be really hard to open that white plastic cap of a new cylinder, which is attached with a nylon string that can cut your hand if you aren't too careful or if you have tugged too hard.

I had a spare cylinder and between both of us, we managed to pant, heave, lug and push it into her home. Then came part two. We tried opening it. We tugged and yanked at the nylon thread. The cap didn't move even an inch. She tried again and then I did. We tried for at least fifteen minutes and gave up. It just wasn't budging. She needed to connect it as she was expecting her mother-in-law and her husband's side of the family in the evening.

'Murphy's Law,' I said.

'Yes, and what an awful day for this to happen! It had to happen only today,' she agreed.

We tried to open it once again, one final attempt, and when we failed, we begrudgingly agreed that we needed a man for the job. Since both our husbands were at work, the only option was to go upstairs to the seventh floor. The seventh floor housed penthouses and many of the posh offices had their service apartments there. Who better to help us than the caretakers there? So we went up and asked the guy who opened the door whether he could help us.

Two ladies, damsels in distress asking for help. I think it would make most men feel macho and most men would help. This smart looking guy was no different and he came downstairs with us. We pointed out the cylinder and he began tugging at the string. He was trying really hard and his face contorted because of the effort. My friend then had a laughter attack seeing him struggle so. She ran out of the kitchen and I could see her almost collapsing on the sofa, behind his back. I could see her stuffing a hanky into her mouth to stop the laughter.

Laughter is really infectious and her crazy behaviour was affecting me too. To my horror, I found myself trying to suppress my laughter while the poor man struggled and panted. I just couldn't hold it in anymore and I was so embarrassed as the guy would think we were laughing at him. Truth be told, we actually were. But we didn't want him to think that.

And to top it, my friend was pointing at his shapely butt which was outlined well as he bent over. That made me crack up even more. I said the first thing that came to my head. 'This gas cylinder does not open up easily. It is as strong as Sylvester Stallone.' And we both burst out into loud raucous guffaws like it was the funniest thing on earth, so relieved that we could explode with laughter.

The guy looked at us with a deadpan expression. He did not even smile. He probably concluded that we were mad and said, 'Madam, *humse nahin hoga. Mein apne boss ko bulaunga*.' (I am not able to do it. I shall ask my boss to help you.)

I managed to thank him.

I had threatened my friend with dire consequences (that included stopping all the tea-sipping chat sessions on the balcony) if she as much dared smile when the boss came. And after two minutes, the boss arrived to help us.

We again pointed out the offending cylinder. He bent over and tugged the string and at that moment, there was a distinct sound that went "prrrrrrrrrrr". To this day, I do not know if it was his trouser ripping or whether it was gas being let out. (And not from the cylinder either.) Exactly at the same time, the string gave way and the man stood up straight triumphantly, mission accomplished. It was enough to send us plummeting into the mad land of laughter. The boss thought we were laughing in joy, and we managed to thank him for helping us.

The moment he went out, we rolled on the floor and I am sure he heard us. I promptly told her that he was hers (and not mine, I emphasised) as he had helped her.

I am certain in fact, that they heard us that day, because after that day, both of them quickly looked the other way if they ran into us in the lobby or while waiting for the elevator or at the parking lot.

I have moved to a different place now, and when I call her up these days, just asking her, 'How is your boss in the penthouse?' is enough to send us both into mad giggles.

You don't realise it when it is happening, but sometimes in life, it is these unexpected gifts like crazy laughing sessions with friends that you long cherish, even years after the moment has passed.

A *floppy story*

In the early nineties, the internet was not as widespread in India as it is now. The technological revolution hadn't yet taken place and 'floppy' meant a disc, and not that which is now defined by the urban dictionary. Computer courses were hailed as the courses of the future.

I was working at a computer education centre, looking after placements. We used to rely on printed reports for our meetings and I had to submit one the next day, at the monthly meeting of all the centres.

It was an important report. I was in a tearing hurry to take a printout. To prevent unauthorised use by the students at the centre, the dot matrix printer that the centre had was located right next to the General Manager's desk and was fiercely guarded by him. That particular day, there were some exams going on and I could not find any computer free to work on. Laptops were a big luxury back then, unlike today. I didn't know what to do. Finally, one of the faculty members told me that he could spare his computer for about fifteen minutes and I could work on it. I jumped at the chance as eagerly as politicians grab the mike when given the chance to speak.

Since the computer I was working on did not have a printer connected to it, I put the contents into a floppy and took it to the machine that was connected to the printer, which was again occupied by another faculty member. I waited for a long time. Finally he finished and said he was going out for a smoke and he logged out.

Relieved that I could finally get my report printed, I sat down to use it to take a printout. I put the floppy in. It did not go in. It was an old machine. So I pushed it a little harder and it obliged. I clicked on the icon which showed the floppy drive. At that precise moment, the screen flickered and went blank. I did not know what to do. I tried retrieving my data. It was futile. With each passing minute, my hopes of catching the usual commuter train home were crushed. I would be late. It was to be a long day.

The General Manager, Mr Shah, was a towering personality; tall, dark, hefty with a huge moustache to boot. On normal days, he intimidated people. On a day like this, I didn't know how he would react if I went to him with this problem. His reactions to people were as unpredictable as the London weather. But that day, he actually offered to help me. Perhaps it was because he saw how distraught I was. I was on the verge of bursting into tears and very desperate to get that printout. A quick glance at my watch told me that I had already missed my train home.

Mr Shah asked me not to worry. He came over to my computer and tried retrieving my data. But he failed to. Then the guy who had gone for a smoke came back. He was supposedly an expert. He too tried and was puzzled.

He then asked me what exactly had happened and when I told him, he said we could try once more by re-inserting the floppy, and restarting the computer.

With that, he pressed the eject button. The floppy seemed to be stuck. He tried taking it out manually, but it was jammed. I was ready to pull out my hair. But the General Manager was determined that I should get my printout. So he summoned the Hardware Engineer. The faculty member who had allowed me to use the machine was giving me a glare and I looked at him helplessly, a bit apologetic that his work was now getting held up because of me.

The Hardware Engineer came in and he opened up the machine. He discovered what the problem was.

He then scratched his head and said, "How in the world did you manage this?"

It was one of the most embarrassing moments of my life. I wished the earth would open up and swallow me. In addition to the floppy already existing in the machine, I had also managed to push in mine. There were now *two* floppies in the same drive! Oh, the horror!

I could see the faculty member shaking his head, suppressing a laugh and the General Manager doing the same thing.

To this day, I don't know how I could have done such a stupid thing. I hate floppies, and I am now glad that pen drives have replaced them. At that time, it seemed like a big deal to me. I was so embarrassed and it seemed like I would not be able to show my face in the office the next day.

But had it happened now, I would have just shrugged and moved on. Most people are too busy leading their own lives to bother about laughing at you.

What seems very important and larger than life to you may not even make a small difference to others. I did not know it then, but I know now that when such things happen, the best thing you can do is join in the laughter.

Free wheelie

This little adventure happened when I was twenty. I was living with my parents in Kochi, Kerala at that time. A cousin of ours who lived in a small town nearby had to board a flight from Kochi. The easiest way for him to reach the airport was by bike. Since the airport at that time did not have a facility where he could be assured that his bike would be safe for a week, for the duration of his trip, he decided to leave it with us. My brother, who was seventeen at that time, hesitatingly asked him if we could use it till he came back. My cousin, being a generous soul, readily agreed. I thought to myself that he was either very trusting or did not care about his bike much or maybe he just did not know how to say no. For my brother and me, it was like manna from heaven. We had a motor bike all to ourselves for a whole week!

My brother, like many boys his age, knew how to handle it with ease. He took me for a couple of rides. We felt so great, so grown up, as we happily rode around the neighbourhood on that bike.

After a couple of rounds, I wasn't content riding pillion anymore and wanted to ride the bike.

'Please show me how to do it,' I begged my brother. At first he refused, but after I worked on him a little, which consisted of me agreeing to do all his allotted chores for a week, like keeping the garbage out, cleaning the table, taking the dogs out for a walk, he agreed to teach me.

The bike had gears that had to be changed with the foot. Whoever heard of such an absurd concept? At least I hadn't! Gears had to be changed with the hand for cars (which were non-automatic) and scooters that I could handle with ease. This one was a new concept for me.

Then you had to look forward and accelerate and release the clutch slowly. In theory, I understood it well.

I mounted the bike. I felt great. Visions of those glamorised bike racing champions came to my mind, and I felt powerful. My brother stood nervously by the side watching me.

'Are you sure you can handle this?' he asked.

'Of course! Don't worry,' I assured him confidently.

After all, he is younger to me and anything he can do, I can do better.

Or so I thought.

I did what he told me to – or at least what I thought he told me to do.

The bike *jumped*, actually jumped into the air four times like a startled toad caught in the headlights of a car at night.

Needless to say, I jumped with it. The sheer fright and shock numbed my senses and I crashed into a banana tree. A bunch of bananas fell and so did the bike and me. And they weren't even ripe!

My parents, my neighbours and even the people who lived behind our house, came running out and I had to be rescued. To add to my shame, I had to lie there under the bike and the tree, till they lifted the tree first, then the bike. My dad, I think, was more concerned that the bananas had fallen before they were ripe. The shouting that they gave me that day still rings in my ears.

I had to do my brother's chores for a week too. A promise is a promise. Neither of us mentioned anything to my cousin when he came back. Fortunately, the only thing damaged in this whole operation was my ego.

That was the end of my trying to learn how to ride a bike.

'Oh God, grant me the courage to accept the things I cannot change, to change the things I can, and the wisdom to know the difference,' goes a prayer.

The older you grow, the more accepting you become. You are willing to be content in the knowledge that there are some things beyond you. Some things that you just can't do. And just because you can't do it, it does not make you inferior in any way.

My ego has accepted it. Or rather, I have browbeaten my ego to accept it, by pacifying it a bit, by repeatedly telling it that I can drive a four wheeler, I can parallel park with ease and I can also drive a two wheeler without a gear and I have great control over a bicycle and I can even ride without holding the handle bars!

But when it comes to geared motor bikes, I prefer admiring them – both the bike and the rider.

And after all these years, I can now proudly say that I have finally learnt how to ride a bike. I drove a 350cc sports bike recently. And guess who my teacher was?

My son! I thought I had closed the bike chapter. But I had thought wrong. Just goes on to show that you should never say never. Things can change in ways you never envisaged.

Vegetable balls

Many years ago – it seems like an alternate lifetime – I was a teacher at a pre-school. I loved my job. There was nothing more I looked forward to each morning than going to school, and being with my students, all in the age group of two to four. As soon as I opened the gate to the school, there would be an army of tiny people, running towards me chanting, 'Preeti Aunty… Preeti Aunty.' I had to hug each one of them before I entered the classroom. I enjoyed working with the children. They were bright, smart, funny and enthusiastic. I can confidently vouch that little children are the most honest people you will ever meet. I was never tired of the kids, and I had a whale of a time, and so did they. There was immense satisfaction in knowing that you were making a difference in the lives of these children.

But if there was one thing that I did not look forward to about my job, it was the parent-teacher meetings. They were exhausting. I had to patiently answer every single question that the parents asked about their child. Parents, especially first timers, can be very inquisitive, wanting to know each and every detail of what their precious angel did at school and how he or she managed without the parent, and what delightful things he or she said. Meeting with each set of parents took about twenty minutes.

Parents in the initial years are completely responsible for moulding their children. After all, they spend only three hours at pre-school and the rest of the time, they are at home. The kind of inputs that a child receives at home makes a big difference. Some parents ruin their children's thinking skills and physical agility by parking them in front of the television for long hours, instead of having a healthy blend of outdoor and indoor activities. The kids really turn into zombies with no ability to imagine and think. I had many such children in my class, and it was easy to spot them.

Of course, I had to smile politely and tactfully convey the message across to the parents. I felt it was important to convey what I felt to the parents. So by the end of these meetings, I would be completely drained out. It took such a humongous effort to refrain from saying what I *really* wanted to.

So, when a friend and her husband offered to pick me up from school after a PTA meet and suggested we have lunch outside, I gratefully accepted and looked forward to meeting both of them. Her husband tells the funniest stories. He is also naturally loud, forthright and the kind of person who will not hesitate to call a spade a spade. He talks very animatedly, using a lot of gestures to get his point across. He was also the country head of his organisation and was a person used to taking charge of things.

He chose a nice Chinese restaurant, which had a pretty garden. We decided to have our meal there as the weather was perfect. Our children were at school and we looked forward to catching up without a thousand interruptions which come with the parent territory.

My friend and I were busy talking. I was telling her about the different kinds of parents that I had to deal with. We told her husband that he could go ahead and place the order for us and he was free to choose whatever he liked. He was hunched over the menu and was studying it intently so he could choose for us two ladies. The waiter came to take the order.

In his booming voice, with a hand gesture to match, my friend's husband asked, 'Do you have balls?'

There was a stunned silence all around. My friend and I looked at each other and burst out laughing. The waiter was trying hard to suppress his laughter too.

Even then he did not realise what he had said. He looked at both of us puzzled and asked, 'What? Don't you like vegetable balls?'

That made us laugh even harder. We could barely speak.

To this day, when I go to a Chinese restaurant and read, 'Vegetable balls in garlic sauce', I cannot help giggling.

And just for the record, I don't like vegetable balls. With or without garlic sauce!

Textually yours

The way we communicate has changed so much over the years. When I was a child, I remember we had to call the telephone exchange and book a 'trunk call' if we had to speak to someone in another city. We had to wait for about 15-20 minutes, after which the telephone exchange would call you back, and connect you to whoever you wanted to speak to.

After that came the era of making STD calls. STD stood for Subscriber Trunk Dialling, and not some awful disease which you got if you had unprotected sex. There sprung telephone booths all over, which proudly announced in huge lettering 'ISD STD PCO', which meant you could make international, national as well as local calls.

Technology progressed some more and then came pagers. Everyone carried these pagers around. They were like mini-bricks and people wore them clipped to their trousers. You could call up a particular number and have a message delivered to the pager. The person could then go to the nearest landline and call you back.

After that came the first mobiles. They too were like bricks, but definitely a huge improvement over the pager. These were not smart phones though and hence the messaging apps that we have today on our smart phones were not as prevalent as they are these days. Sending text messages was how we communicated. We had "sms packs" for texting. For Rs.99/-, we could send unlimited messages.

If you have used these sms packs for sending text messages, chances are you have probably had an oops-i-just-text-messaged-the-wrong-person-moment. Maybe several.

I have had several such moments over the years. I am usually careful, but sometimes, (okay, many times) I have sent wrong messages to the wrong people – or maybe the right messages to the wrong people or even wrong messages to right people. They have provided me with laughs most of the time, embarrassment sometimes, and a resolve to be more careful in future, each and every time.

I have declared to my father's friend who is about eighty-five that I love him and miss him a lot, thinking that I am sending the message to my mom. He does not pick up my calls anymore.

I have told my car mechanic that I am waiting for him outside school and asked him where the hell he is, and to come fast, thinking that I was messaging my friend who I was supposed to meet, after picking up the kids from school. He replied promptly, 'Which school?' and two seconds later, 'Who are you?' I still squirm in embarrassment and then laugh whenever I think of it.

I have declared to a good friend that I have dropped my daughter at the dance class and I am dying to talk to him, but everyone will be around and so we cannot really have a heart to heart chat, thinking that I was messaging one of my closest women friends. He politely informed me of my blunder.

I have asked a friend who lives in another city to come inside right now or else I am going to come out there and drag her in, thinking that I was messaging my husband who was just outside my house and was talking to some neighbours, while I was waiting for him to come indoors so I could switch on the movie that we were supposed to be watching together.

I have called my paediatrician a fool and a smart ass, thinking that I was messaging my brother. He texts back saying, 'Who is this?' I was elated, pleased and overjoyed that while I was filling up the forms at his office I had given only my landline number and not my mobile number.

I have told the bus driver of my children's school bus that I am there for him, if he feels like talking, thinking that I was sending it to a friend who was going through a divorce. Poor guy must have collapsed reading it, considering the fact that the caller tune which greets you when you call him is "*Om jai jagadeesh hare*".

I have messaged a random stranger telling him I have got a really nice perfume for him. He messaged back saying, 'What brand?' It was an expensive brand, and it was only after I replied that I realised I was not talking to my son. I promptly blocked the guy.

I have been at the receiving end of such messages too. I once got a message asking if I can drop off the beers. I replied, 'No, I drank them all.'

Another time I got a message saying, 'He just left. You can come over.' I replied, 'No, he is waiting around the corner to catch you.'

One time the phone buzzed thrice. It was the same message being sent asking where I was. 'Outside your door now, and before that I was peeping through your bathroom window when you showered,' I replied. I wonder what must have happened to the recipient after that.

I would all the time get calls for a person named Ali.

'Ali? *Kaise ho?*' they would ask.

I would change my voice and say that Ali has migrated to Dubai or Canada or whatever country came to my head.

Now we have instant messaging apps as well as Caller ID apps that show you who is calling simply by the number. You can also see whether the message has been read, at what time and also if the person is online. Sending messages in error rarely happens as the DP (display picture) of the person makes it clearer. Smart phones have certainly made life easier. But they have also taken away the laughs we can get out of wrongly sent messages.

The uninvited visitor

It was 2007, and the grief was raw, as I had just lost my beloved father. I had also started a blog sometime in October 2006. I would write every single day. I would focus only on the positive or funny things in my life, as grief threatened to engulf me. Eventually, over time, I made a set of great blogging pals from all over the world. My blogging community welcomed me with open arms and open minds. I had never met a set of cooler people. There were many blogs that I read at that time, from all over the world. I knew them not only by their blog names – Tim, Katherine, Niall, Sue, Mr Fab, Rayne, Gawpo – but I also had spoken to some of them over Skype. Oh, the power of technology! I made friends with people from Portugal, Arkansas, Sweden, Italy and many more countries. Many of their blogs have ceased to exist now, but we have remained friends over social media. In fact, I have also met some of them when I travelled to their countries.

Since I was always on the lookout for material for my blog those days, I thought in terms of blog posts. Any event that occurred in my life would immediately go through an analysis as to whether it could be converted into an interesting blog post. What is to follow was written after one such incident, where I had an uninvited visitor, who took me by surprise.

◆

I had a guest the other day. He crept in uninvited. And the audacious, shameless, brazen guy that he was, he decided to surprise me, in my bathroom. Can you believe it?

He was waiting for me when I went in. Luckily, I spotted him before undressing and getting into the shower. My first instinct was to scream – real loud. My heart was in my mouth, pounding. But I controlled myself and had a closer look at him. He stared back. He didn't say a word. He did not move either.

'Wow. This would truly be a scoop on my blog,' was the thought that occurred to me. Yes, even in that shell-shocked, half-dazed, adrenalin-induced hazy state of mind, the first thing that occurred to me was my blog. And, I deny that I am addicted to my blog. Does anyone know "Blogaholic Anonymous"? Not that I need help or anything. I mean, I do think of other things apart from my blog – like Niall's blog or Sue's blog – or Mr Fab's blog or Tim's blog or Rayne's or Katherine's.

But I digress. To come back to the story, I quickly whipped out my phone and clicked a few pictures. The guy still hadn't moved. He was still staring at me. That was when I decided to scream. It was mostly for effect. It was also to test whether my husband knew of my existence while watching television. He is mostly unaware of anything but the drama or game unfolding on the screen. I have to assert myself every now and then. Just because I'm quiet doesn't mean I am gone.

So I let out my best imitation of the scream I remember hearing in *Psycho*. He was upstairs in precisely six seconds. Satisfied and happy, I pointed out the visitor to him. He took one look at him, shut the bathroom door and said, 'Well, I am scared too,' and went back to watching television! And no, I am not making this up. My two children are witness to this incident.

After that, I had no choice but to approach a security guard from our complex. He puffed up his chest in pride, and accompanied me all the way to my house. He then managed to cajole the visitor into a laundry basket. He snapped on the lid, and then transported him away from my home, and released him. All this was in view of about seventeen neighbourhood kids and a few adults! My *Psycho* scream had even more effect than I had imagined!

An attentive audience had gathered to watch the proceedings. They accompanied him on the great march to freedom and watched in wonder as he opened the basket and released the garden lizard.

◆

Now, a different view of the same story and this time, it is from the garden lizard's point of view.

I've always lived in the garden. I was born here, raised here and I lead a comfortable existence. There is enough food, water and lovely greenery. There are a lot of plants where I can hide. However, I have always wondered what goes on inside that tall brick structure. At nights, for a few hours, the place comes alive. There is music, there is screaming. A woman's voice which keeps going on about something called homework. After a while, some delicious aromas waft out from inside and there is the gentler sound of humans conversing.

Some more time elapses and then it all goes quiet and dark. After that there is silence. I have been watching this forever now and I have had enough of looking in from the outside. I simply cannot watch anymore. I have to go inside and discover this new world for myself. I have decided that I want to be an explorer.

I get inside through a magical opening in the wall which is sometimes there and sometimes not there. It is mostly not there after the sunset, when the woman yells, 'Shut the windows, the mosquitoes will come in.'

As soon as I enter this new world through this magical opening, I see a huge structure with wooden legs. There is something soft on it, covered with a cloth. I peer cautiously. It certainly doesn't look good to climb on. So I venture further in. I am scared. But I also want to see what lies ahead. There are no plants to hide behind. In case of danger, I am completely exposed. Oh well. I will take my chances. I haven't come this far for nothing.

There is this little white thing and it gives me some kind of a shelter. It has a very strong smelling little solid wet thing inside it. I don't want to climb into it, as it looks slippery and so I decide to go behind it. Just as I am settling into a comfortable position, suddenly without warning, an enormous creature with two legs walks in. I think this is the female human whose voice I hear every night. She screams. She points something strange at me, and it goes 'click-click' thrice, while some kind of light coming out from it blinds me temporarily. Then she vanishes. I am really scared now. But there is no opening now for me to escape back into my world. I remember the sun has set. Damn! I should have done this a little earlier. So I would still have the opening to get back through. I regret my little adventure now. But there does not seem to be an escape route and there is nothing I can do but wait.

I wait with my heart pounding. Another human appears very briefly through the larger magical opening. Then he too vanishes almost as quickly as he appears. By this time I am desperately looking for more places to hide. I wish there were some plants here. I now wish I had never ventured in. All of a sudden there are lots of human voices. They sound like baby humans. I decide to keep quiet and scare them if they come near. But, wait – here is a new human – he has something in his hand. He doesn't seem to be scared of me. Help! He has caught me now and I am inside a huge prison, with no way out. The prison is moving. I am moving wildly inside it. I am trapped and there is no escape. I am certain this is the last I'll see of my garden.

Suddenly the moving stops. The prison is open. I wait for a second and scamper to safety. I can see all the baby humans watching me. I look *around. It is going to take me a while to find my way back home — but at least I'm alive!*

◆

After this incident, I always double check before I have a bath. You never know what you might find in there. Who would have imagined a garden lizard in the bathroom! I am now glad it wasn't a snake. Had it been, then the scream would have been for real.

This incident makes me think that sometimes when things do not go the way you want them to, or when someone does not behave in a manner you expect them to, or even when someone unexpectedly turns up where they are not supposed to be, it might momentarily give you a jolt. But what always helps is when you look at it from the other person's point of view. We begin to get greater clarity then, and we become more willing to accept situations beyond our control.

It happened one night

Ninety-eight percent of the time, my husband is sweet. Really sweet. Not the sticky-sweet like cheap candy-chocolates that adhere stubbornly to every crevice in your mouth, but genuine sweet like a Godiva chocolate whose taste lingers long after you have finished relishing it.

The other two percent of the time, he watches television. Therefore I was gobsmacked, when he kicked me one night. Yes, he did. No, I am not making it up. It wasn't when he was watching TV either.

I did not know what hit me. Literally. Because I was asleep at that time. One moment I was warm, cosily snuggled up in the quilt, dreaming of a wonderful vacation in Spain where I had been sent on an assignment by a travel company, and the next moment, I was on the cold floor, befuddled, with excruciating pain shooting up my sides.

'Fut the Wuk!' I yelled and sleep made a hasty exit from my head, like orange pips spat out in disgust.

I looked at my husband. He was not watching television and he still looked sweet. His eyes were closed, and he was frowning in his sleep.

I grabbed his blanket and yanked it off, having discovered through years of sharing the marital bed, that this is the quickest way to have him awake.

It was his turn to be surprised.

'What?' he asked, still sweetly. It is hard to make him lose his cool.

'You should be answering that. You just kicked me and I fell off the bed,' I said.

There was stunned silence. He was as shocked as I had been. Then he apologised profusely and we both burst into laughter. Then he explained.

The organisation which my husband had been working for, had come out with a scheme, where for a certain amount which would be deducted from your salary, you could upgrade your car. If you didn't want anything to be deducted, they would still give you a brand new car, but it would be a standard one, not a luxury car.

Every one upgraded.

He had been dreaming of his ex-boss. His ex-boss is straight out of *Devil Wears Prada,* only male. He was pleased when you sucked up to him, stole credit for your work and then gave you a lousy rating, no matter how hard you worked. You could never please him.

His ex-boss chose not to pay and went in for a Maruti Suzuki Wagon R. My husband opted for a Hyundai Accent, a higher end model. This was the time when Accent had just been launched in India, and owning one made heads turn.

When my husband drove to work and parked beside his ex-boss' Wagon R, his ex-boss just couldn't bear it.

'I didn't know you were a Punjabi,' he sarcastically told my husband, in a disguised sugar-coated voice. (My husband isn't one.)

'Why?' asked my husband, genuinely surprised.

'No – it is usually the Punjabis who show off and go for big flashy cars,' he said.

Now, sweetness is not to be confused with sharpness and razor sharp wit. My husband has both and his repartees were one of the reasons why I had fallen in love with this man, many years ago. It quickly came to his aid.

In a deadpan voice he said, 'No, I am not a Punjabi. There are three reasons why I have bought this car. One – I truly believe it is a great car. Two – I think you are young only once, and if you are able to afford and enjoy the good things, you should go for it. Three – unlike you, I do not intend retiring from this company and when I look for a job outside, I can factually say that my last company gave me an Accent, and therefore they will have to better that.'

His ex-boss sank into his chair and began to look busy. He did not say a word.

The night he kicked me, he had just dreamt that he was at the beach, relaxing with all of us, when his ex-boss arrived there in a rusty old car. When he saw all of us, he began throwing sand on our new car. My husband was livid, and dreamt that he was kicking him hard, which explains how I landed up on the floor that night.

It has been about six years now. We both still laugh heartily when we reminisce about that night when he kicked me in his sleep. The laughter, even after all these years, is tinged with that undercurrent of supreme satisfaction that comes when you outsmart a really terrible boss.

Today we are older and hopefully wiser. We have realised that what car you drive does not really matter. There is always going to be somebody with a bigger and a better car. There are also going to be people who cannot afford to buy a car.

Just like there will always be bosses who are rude, haughty and arrogant. One cannot change them. Trying to get the better of them will only be like, to use an old saying, 'wrestling with a pig'. At the end of it, you both are exhausted and filthy and the pig actually enjoys it.

We have learnt that it is best to be like the duck that goes with the flow. To float along the river effortlessly, enjoying the gentle flow of the water and to treat barbs and insults thrown at you, like the 'water off a duck's back'.

And as for that kick in the night – I am waiting for the day, when I can return the favour. It hasn't happened yet.

HEY BROTHER!

"Siblings fight, pull each other's hair, steal stuff, and accuse each other indiscriminately.

But siblings also know the undeniable fact that they are the same blood, share the same origins, and are family.

Even when they hate each other.

And that tends to put all things in perspective."

—Vera Nazarian

Mummy loves me more

My two children are no different from most siblings. They fight, tease each other, bicker, play together and have their own secret language, which all siblings who are close do. Sometimes I eavesdrop on their conversation when they think I am not listening. I enjoy it immensely.

Overheard some time back (when they were twelve and sixteen):

My son to my daughter: You know what, mummy loves me more.

My daughter: Of course not, she loves us both equally.

My son: No, she doesn't. They haven't told you, you are actually adopted.

My daughter paused for a few seconds. I held my breath.

Then she said, "At least they *chose* me, but they are stuck with you."

I am smiling as I write this, and this one is straight going into the memory box.

Barbies, Math and babysitting service

Sometimes you want something very badly. You crave for it so much that it almost consumes you. You wait for years for it, dream of it, bide your time, and pray desperately to realise what you wish for. When it finally becomes a reality, your life changes in ways you never even imagined. You just cannot believe your luck. The birth of my daughter was one such moment for me.

Since I already had a little boy, I desperately wanted a baby girl. But hoping for a combination of a boy *and* a girl seemed to be expecting too much. And even though my husband and I badly wanted a girl, we comforted ourselves saying, even if it was a boy, we would be okay. 'Let's just pray for a healthy baby, boy or girl,' I said and my husband agreed.

Deep down, I dreaded it – if I had a boy a second time, there would be three males in the house and I would be the sole representative of my tribe. Long before I had children, I used to longingly look at all the frilly frocks, pretty bows and a hundred other things on display in windows of shops that you could dress up a baby girl with and used to hope that someday I would get a chance to buy all that.

I will never forget that moment when I gave birth to my little doll and the nurse held her up and said, 'It's a baby girl.' I was overwhelmed. I had opted for a natural birth without any epidural or painkillers whatsoever, so you can imagine the state I must have been in. And in case you're not a mother, yes, it *is* just like they show in the movies! I burst into tears. I was ecstatic!

But in a country like India, it was misinterpreted and two nurses quickly told me, 'No, no, don't cry; you can try for a boy next year.'

I was gobsmacked.

'I already have a boy,' I replied through gritted teeth. (My blood boils when I think of female infanticide. How can people be so *blind, so cruel?*)

I enjoyed both my children immensely while they were growing up. They were different from each other. He was the archetypal older brother. He teased her but also protected her and found her to be very cute too. She was the epitome of the stereotype of what people think girls like. She loved pink. Everything had to be pink. She loved frills, laces and make-up and braiding long hair. Her favourite subjects at school were Math, English and Art.

She was a lot like me in some ways, but also very different from me. When I was growing up, I hated anything frilly. I was a tomboy. But I loved Art, Math and writing.

There was one area where she and I were at the opposite ends of the spectrum and that was when it came to Barbie dolls. I loathe Barbies, but she loved them! She had fourteen Barbies, all of them were gifts. One of her favourite childhood games, when she was about six or seven years old, was "Barbie-Barbie". She would insist that I play "Barbie-Barbie" with her. That mostly consisted of her taking out her Barbies, changing their outfits and accessories and lining them up, combing their hair, etc. I soon got tired of it. But my daughter was merciless.

'Please, mama. One more game of "Barbie-Barbie",' she would insist.

I did not have the heart to refuse.

So mostly to entertain myself, I told her that we would have to make "Barbie-Barbie" more interesting. She agreed and came up with the idea of a babysitting service.

We assumed different identities for the "Barbie-Barbie" game and for some reason we always assumed English names as they seemed more apt. In our game, I was a busy author who had no time for her children, three hideous-looking Barbies named Jo-Ann, Beth and Molly May. I had to rush off to my editorial meetings all the time, and hence I leave them at a very good childcare which is run efficiently by her.

This entire scenario was her creation totally. I just played along. She also had a toy-pony and she gave rides to my children. The name of her childcare changed each time we played the game. Sometimes it was "Happy-land babysitting". At other times it was "Magic hours babysitting service". On some days, it was just "Purvi babysitting service". The names she came up with depended on her mood.

'Hello there,' I would say in a proper English accent. 'Can you take care of my three children for me? I have an important meeting in London and will be gone for at least a couple of hours.'

'Of course, ma'am. No problem at all. We would love to. We even have a pony ride,' she would reply.

So I would leave my "children" in her able care and I would "drive to London" for my important meeting.

It gave a little respite from the "Barbie-Barbie" game, and it bought me a little time, which I would use to do the dishes, or cook or do the laundry or clean the house.

When I came back to collect my children, I would tell her, 'So, your rates, as advertised in the *Telegraph* are 7.50 pounds an hour. I have left three children for four hours now. How much do I owe you?'

My heart would fill with pride as I saw her calculating and giving me the right answer. Since she was good at Math, I would step up the challenge a bit more. I would also add rates for the pony rides. I would say, 'Three children. Jo-Ann had four rides, Beth had only two and Molly May is a little greedy, so I know she would have had seven. So how much do I pay for the pony rides please?'

Depending on her ability to calculate, I would integrate simple fractions and decimals and multiplication into the game and vary the figures. She would make a bill. 'It's an invoice,' I would tell her and she would write it as I spelled it out. Then she would hand it over to me. I would pay her with play-money and I would collect my children and go home. The children couldn't wait to go back to babysitting as I neglected them at home and they had so much fun at the babysitting service. So I used the babysitting service very often.

She was happy that Mummy had played "Barbie-Barbie" with her. I was happy that it was time well spent, and more importantly, that she practised her Math.

As the years went by, she needed me less and less. Now she is all set to go to another country for her college. She still has all her Barbies in a box in the loft. I asked her if she remembered her Barbie babysitting days. She did and we laughed so much recalling them.

'How clever you were, mama,' she said.

'Not cleverer than you my darling,' I replied.

The perfect child

My daughter always has stories to share when she comes back from school. She, to this day, insists that I have to put away whatever I happen to be working on, and give her my complete and undivided attention as she narrates in great detail, what happened that day. She is also a good mimic and often has me in splits. Sometimes she is agitated and then after she talks to me about it, she feels better.

I always learn a lot from her. We treasure those moments – she and I. She is a lot like me, we have the same sense of humour, and we are completely in sync. It is hard to stop us once we get started. She reminds me of myself when I was her age, and yet in many ways, she is very different from me.

She was about eleven, when this happened. She came home and had a story to share. It was about this girl in her class who was a perfect student. She never forgot her homework, was always on time, never missed school, studied well for all the tests, and was the epitome of efficiency – a model student, my daughter informed me. I wondered what parenting tricks her father and mother could be using to get their daughter to be this efficient. But I didn't make any comment.

'You know what she told me the other day, Ma?' said my daughter, almost in disbelief.

'What?'

'She said, *I think I will get ninety-nine and three fourths in Math. If I lose that quarter mark, I think I will kill myself.*'

'Good Lord. Is she that good at studies?'

'Yes, and very stuck up too. She always scores 19/20 and 20/20 in all the tests. And she is such a cry baby.'

'What do you mean cry baby?'

'She actually bawls. Can you imagine? If someone tells her even a little thing like "your plait is coming loose", she bawls and weeps like the world is going to end.'

'Oh! She must be a sensitive child then.'

'No ma, not sensitive. She is just a drama queen. She just wants everything to go her way and she cannot accept it if it doesn't. So she cries and bawls to get her way.'

'Oh.'

I didn't know what to say to that. The thought that crossed my mind was – what was the point of being so good at academics if one didn't have a balanced personality? But of course, like a good Indian mother, I said nothing. After all, which Indian parent doesn't aspire for a child who scores perfect marks in exams? I kept my silence.

But the story wasn't over.

'But I made her all right, Ma. She is okay now,' my daughter announced.

'Oh. How?' I asked, my curiosity really piqued.

'She has been sitting next to me for about four months now.'

'And?'

'Now she scores only 14/20 and 16/20. And she doesn't cry anymore.'

Older brothers and inner peace

We have a simple rule in our family. We eat our meals together.

Having dinner together every night is a ritual we have followed as far back as I can remember. On weekends, we have every meal together. Eating in front of the television isn't allowed in our home. We sit down at the dining table to eat. No phones, books or any other distractions are allowed. We have our set places too. Both my husband and I think this is very important to do as a family. If we happen to have guests staying over, they join in as well and we all eat together.

It is usually at meal times that a lot of conversations take place. Sometimes they are funny. Sometimes profound and sometimes there is silence. We always express gratitude for the food that we are eating and count our blessings before we eat.

I remember, during one such meal at the dining table a few years back – my daughter looked glum.

'What happened?' I asked her, knowing her proclivity for drama and mentally preparing myself to what action to take after determining how serious the matter actually would be, in the larger scheme of things. I was used to this, due to years of parenting. Some things needed immediate action. Some appeared to be a storm, but would blow over.

But what she said that day surprised me.

'I desperately need inner peace,' she said solemnly.

That was a first. I was taken aback, but quickly recovered.

'Eat up all your peas. Then they will be inside you and you will have inner peas,' I smiled, feeling very pleased with my smug reply, pointing to the peas *pulav* that we were having.

That brought a smile to my daughter's face and she did not miss the pun or the joke.

'Mama, you always make me smile,' she said.

'I am glad. But where in the world did you get a concept like inner peace? How can you need inner peace, you are only eleven!' I couldn't help exclaiming, part in admiration, part in a "kids-these-days" way.

My daughter revelled in the moment, happy at having got me thinking. But it was brief moment.

'Mom, don't be so impressed with her. She has just been watching too much *Kung-fu Panda* and that is where she got it from,' said my fifteen-year-old son.

I didn't know what to say.

I smiled, recalling many such moments in my own childhood, when my brother and I had these 'I-will-tell-mummy' moments.

These are the treasured memories that we still talk about, as adults, many years later and we laugh.

I felt happy that my children were creating a few such treasures of their own.

Spies, underwear and other things

'Mom, are you a spy?' was the question my seven-year-old greeted me with when I picked her up from school that day. This was a few years back, when we were living in the UK.

For a moment I was stumped. Then I realised that it probably had something to do with the History lessons that they were being taught. I had grown up learning about the Battle of Panipat and memorising the dates when each battle took place. I remember proudly memorising the names of the six Mughal emperors and their eras — starting with Babur, Humayun, Akbar, Jahangir, Shah Jahan and finally Aurangzeb, and the last Mughal Bahadur Shah Zafar. I read with great interest about Bhagat Singh and Chandrashekhar Azad and Jhansi *ki* Rani. Growing up in India, we all knew about the Salt Satyagraha and how Gandhiji got thrown out of a train. It stirred my patriotic fervour and in our playtime, we enacted scenes from Mangal Pandey's life, vowing to kick out the British.

At that time, I never even remotely dreamt that I would live in Britain, in a small town and would be sending my children to a local English school. They loved the place, their school and all their English friends. They had also learnt to speak in a British accent, and it never failed to surprise me how they could switch effortlessly between a British accent and an Indian one, when they came home. Their knowledge of Indian History was limited to what I had taught them. And whenever we visited India, I made sure to take them to all the historical monuments like Akbar's tomb and other places. To my children, all of it was exotic. They were more familiar with British History.

I recalled that a few days earlier, my daughter had mentioned that she had been taught about the Morrison and Anderson shelters. They were air-raid shelters which people needed during the World War II, to protect themselves from the bombs being dropped by German aircrafts. When the night raids became very frequent, people just took to spending whole nights in a shelter. Anderson shelters, made from corrugated iron sheets, bolted together, were half buried in the ground with earth heaped on top of them, to protect them from the blasts. Morrison shelters were made of very heavy steel and could be put in the living room and used as a table. One wire side lifted up for people to crawl underneath and get inside them. My daughter used to make Morrison shelters with the help of bedsheets, the dining table and a little imagination.

But her question on spies was something that stumped me completely. My knowledge of the word was limited to *Spy versus Spy* which I had read in MAD comics while growing up. So there was only one explanation as to why she was asking me if I was a spy.

'Did you learn about spies today?' I asked her.

'Yes,' a bright nod.

'And what did you learn?' I prodded as we began our walk back from school to home.

'Everything that is there to know,' she said with great conviction.

'Really? Everything?' I was fifty percent amused and a hundred percent sceptical.

'Of course. We watched a movie about it. Should I explain it to you?'

'Yes, please.'

She had my entire attention now.

'Look ma,' she said, as though I was the seven-year-old, 'Spies can look exactly like ordinary people. For example, you may look like Preeti Shenoy. You may dress like her and talk like her. You may even be her – but you could be a spy. Which is why I asked if you were a spy.'

There was only one way to answer that.

'Hmm,' I said, '*Maybe* I am a spy. What do you think?'

'Let me see,' she said. Then she tugged my hair.

'Ouch – what did you do that for?'

'To check if it's real hair or a wig.'

'Even if it is real, going by what you said, I could still be a spy.'

I reminded her that she had said that even if I did not look it, I could still be a spy even if I wasn't wearing obvious disguises like a wig and sun glasses.

She paused for a moment and declared with certainty, 'You can never be a spy, ma.'

'Why?' I asked, doing a quick mental comparison of myself with Mata Hari.

'Because, spies don't wash their babies' underwear!' she exclaimed. She was at that age when she still referred to herself and her eleven-year-old brother as my babies, *especially* when she wanted to get something out of me.

'And how do you know I wash your underwear?' I persisted.

'Simple,' she said, 'Otherwise they would stink.'

I smiled. I had no retort to that. Then I asked her, 'What do you think I do the whole day when you are at school, apart from washing your underwear?'

'You write books and do housework and cook and you think about us and papa and wait for us to come back.'

I hugged her then.

In my treasured mental memory storage chest, where I file moments to remember, this one certainly was a gem.

It is lovely to learn new things – be it British history or Indian. And no history lesson in the world can teach you what I learnt that day – that real spies don't wash their babies' underwear.

Feeling needed

Being needed is an inherent human trait. All of us like to be needed. It gives us an ego-kick and a sense of importance. It makes us feel wanted and useful. It makes us feel that we matter. When you are a parent, this is more pronounced than ever, with your little babies completely dependent on you for every need. Oh the joy, the satisfaction and the terrifying realisation that you are now completely responsible for another tiny human.

But with the passage of time, things change. Children grow up and leave home. Many of my friends have been privy to the 'empty nest' syndrome. I have no idea whether I will suffer as badly as they did, or whether I will cope better. I will soon know, as both my children are now set to move to another country, for their college education. I am slowly learning to let go.

When I first watched the 2014 movie *Boyhood* by Richard Linklater, a beautiful time-lapse study of a boy from age five to eighteen, I could completely relate to the mother as she watched her children growing up, and finally leaving home. There is an emotionally charged scene in the movie, where she breaks down a little disappointed, wondering if 'this is all there is' to parenthood.

The thing about parenting is that we forget how little our children were, very quickly. For me, it seems just like the other day when my children were babies, and now they are adults already. Children grow up so fast and stop depending on parents after a certain age. Then they depend on their friends. It may not be wrong to say that after a while, it is the parents who need the kids more than the now grown-up adult children. The bond gets nurtured only by the efforts one puts in. If you have invested in making your bond a close one, chances are it will remain so, even into adulthood.

Most seasoned parents – and by 'seasoned' I mean parents who have two kids or more who are older than five years, until which time you are just a novice – swear that there are laws of the universe conspiring to make their progeny as different as possible from each other. As a seasoned parent, I can vouch it is true. If one likes Bollywood numbers, the other will like rap. If one wants the AC turned off, the other will want it at the highest possible setting. If one child likes pizzas and burgers, the other will usually prefer fresh vegetables and low calorie health food. Yes, there are kids like that! One of my friend's daughters is six and wants to eat only healthy food and insists on five servings of vegetables and fruits a day.

Some of the most cherished memories are the ones made when your children were dependent on you. It is a place you can never go back to. I have many such moments, and I have mostly captured them either on my blog, or in my private journals. I want to share with you one such treasured moment.

My daughter, when she was a child, was an early bird. As though that wasn't enough, she was an eager-beaver as well. Bright-eyed, bushy-tailed, up at the crack of dawn – with her chirpiness directly proportional to the earlier hour – she would fetch a book from our large collection.

Her sleep patterns were in direct contrast to mine, as I usually go to bed only at 1:00 am. My daughter would proceed to convert my back into a sofa, at around 5.30am most mornings. I was too exhausted to protest. My sleeping on my tummy gave her the added advantage of folding up my legs, and making them her backrest, and with a few pillows, she would comfortably settle down. She would then proceed to read aloud. My strict instructions to her were, 'You are *not* allowed to wake mama, no matter what.'

5:30 am is midnight for me. I have threatened her, cajoled her, begged her, pleaded with her and even tried sleeping with cotton stuffed in my ears – but it was futile.

'Maaaaaa … Maaaaaa…' she would say in a sweet honey-coated voice – which in reality is delightful but at 5:15 am in the morning it is more saccharine, less sugar. 'What is this word?' she would ask.

I would refuse to answer.

'I am not waking you up, maaa. I just want you to tell me one word. I am getting stuck, you see and it is FIRST-ating.'

She wasn't one to give up easily.

No, thank you! I don't see and I don't want to see.

So I would mumble asking her to spell it. Usually the word would be one with an apostrophe or something that is hyphenated. In such cases, even a simple word like 'I'd' becomes ID when the apostrophe is not read out. So I would mumble something to the effect of not knowing what it is and would desperately plead with her to let me sleep for ten more minutes.

At this point, she would stick the book about two centimetres away from my eyes.

'Maaaa, just have a look one time. If you tell me what it is just once, I promise I will let you sleep.'

Deal sealed, I would grudgingly open one eye and read out the word. After precisely one and a half minutes – just at that point when I was drifting off to blissful sleep, she would tap me and say, 'Maaa… Are ten minutes over yet?'

After several days of this, I had a brainwave. I finally hatched a plan to fix that problem. At least I presumed I did. I had no idea what I was in for.

I taught her how to measure how much a minute is. I taught her to say, 'One thousand one... One thousand two... One thousand three, and so on... up to one thousand sixty.' It would take approximately a minute. And for ten minutes, she had to say it ten times. She understood perfectly and nodded delightedly at the new discovery.

The next morning, in addition to 'Maaaa... What word is this?' I also had to listen to her shouting, 'One thousand one, one thousand two...' at the top of her voice at 5.30 am.

I asked her why she did not ever bother my husband. I asked why she did not wake him up for a change. Why did he get away scot free?

'Aww mummy,' she replied, 'Papa will never wake up. You always tell me what I want to know. Look ma, if I knew how to read, I would not bother you.'

You can't argue with logic like that. And secretly, I did enjoy it while it lasted.

Now that she will soon be off to college, all I can do is reminiscence and relive those moments through the pages of this book.

A little gift

They say blood is thicker than water. There indeed is something special about the connection that you share with your siblings – no matter how fractured or how strong it is when you are adults. Like me, if you hail from a time when it was the norm to have two or three children, then you would probably agree wholeheartedly about the importance of growing up with siblings. I know many who were raised as single children, but who have gone on to have two children as adults, as they say that they longed for a brother or a sister while growing up, and they do not want their children to experience the same.

My brother and I share a close bond, like many siblings do. Research has proved that the sibling relationship has the power to influence who we are and what we turn into as adults. Many of my friends admit to a big influence that their older sibling had in influencing their choice of career.

I fail to understand how even such a deep bond becomes diluted when tainted with money. There are many cases of fights over property, businesses and other material things. How do siblings turn into enemies? Why does greed consume everything?

Why don't we remember that no matter how much money you have or you don't have, you still need four pallbearers to carry you on your last journey, and one of them would most probably be your sibling? Fights over property then seem so futile.

Childhood memories are the foundation of the bond that you share with your sibling. The behaviour patterns we establish in childhood get carried forward into our adult lives too. There are many memories that I cherish which I share with my brother. But the one that we still talk about whenever we meet is this one.

It was a long time ago, when kids still collected postage stamps and sea shells from the beach. What I owned was a prized possession – a triangular-shaped postage stamp, with a beautiful picture of a rocket on it. The country was Mongolia. It raised my status among my peers, the other kids, as all of us were philatelists – tiny stamp collectors.

'She has a triangular stamp.'

'Really? Triangular?'

'Yes.'

'From Mongolia!'

'Can we please have a look at it?'

The awe and reverence that single stamp evoked, increased my status among the other children. Whenever I took out the stamp album, I felt like a queen. Nobody else had a triangular postage stamp. Nor stamp with a picture of a rocket on it, for that matter. It was rare those days.

My brother used to longingly look at it. I wouldn't even let him touch my coveted stamp album. It was safely locked and the key deposited with mom, if I wasn't around.

My brother was not one to give up so easily. What he wanted, he usually got. He waited for a chance. Patiently.

It came when we were returning from school one day. I was with a friend, walking ahead and he was trailing behind us, as usual.

The green raw mangoes hanging in Mr Sharma's garden, just above his gate, were irresistible. Anyone who has eaten sour green mangoes will know just how much they tempt.

My friend suggested that we pluck a few. She and I climbed the gate, reached out, and started plucking the green mangoes. What we did not anticipate was Mrs Sharma's hawk-like watch over her precious mangoes.

'Hey, you thieves!' she roared. And then a second later, 'I know you. You are Mr Kamath's daughter, aren't you?'

I was terrified that she had recognised me. I had no idea that she knew my father, and also knew me. I did not answer. Instead, we climbed down and ran for our dear lives, carrying the mangoes with us. We did not slow down till we reached the bus stop.

Then we burst into laughter, as we had escaped and we had a bounty as well.

My brother had been a silent observer. 'Here!' I held out a green mango.

He looked at it for a second. His mouth watered at the sight. But he shook his head.

'No,' he said. Then, he uttered the dreaded words, 'I will tell Mom what you did today.'

'Please, please, please, don't,' I begged, pleaded.

We knew what was in store if our mom found out that I had *stolen* mangoes. That too, from someone whom they knew.

When we reached home, I asked my mother for the key, to take out my stamp album. She was surprised when she saw me giving my coveted Mongolia rocket stamp to my brother.

'But why?' my mother asked in surprise. 'Just like that, Ma. I felt like giving him a gift.'

Later, that day, the phone rang.

It was Mrs Sharma, asking to speak to my mother.

Miaow, miaow,
I love you

'Don't go to Egypt in June. Nobody goes in June – it is blistering hot,' was the horrified response that I got from people when they heard about the trip we had planned. It was an ambition of a lifetime, a long-cherished dream to be able to go to the land of Pharaohs. Everything was in place, the itinerary, the tickets, the dates for the kids' summer holidays, and most importantly, the affordable off-season rates. So a little thing like the weather seemed the least of the impediments and off we went.

Travelling to a place which you have never visited before is the best way to teach children about culture, history and to introduce them to a world which is completely new. Of course, the same holds true for adults as well. Over the years, we have travelled to many places and have created many happy memories. We have done things off the beaten path, and had many adventures as well as some scary moments – like narrowly escaping being gored to death by a baby elephant and also forgetting our very expensive Nikon D-80 in a crowded restaurant and running through the streets of York in UK like madmen to retrieve it. But those adventures I shall leave for another day. This one that happened in Egypt still makes us smile. My daughter was about seven and my son was about ten.

The first thing that struck me as we drove out of Cairo airport was a sense of *déjà vu*. I soon realised why – the buildings, the architecture, the well laid-out roads and the planned greenery looked just like Chandigarh, back in India! Soon it gave way to typical Cairo cityscape. What struck me was the unfinished exteriors of occupied residential buildings, left purposely so, with exposed bricks, which we were told was commonly done, to avoid the heavy tax that owners of 'finished buildings' had to pay. They were interspersed by magnificent mosques, splashed with all shades of brown, much like the desert sand. Finally as we drove towards the old town, the pyramids emerged magnificently in the background, almost like magic. We clutched each other in excitement at the sight, which was so familiar due to the numerous photos, movies and books, all featuring them. Being at the actual spot felt surreal, like we had stepped into a postcard or a movie set.

After we had explored Cairo and satiated ourselves spending a whole day at the pyramids, we flew to Aswan, from where we were to take a cruise along the River Nile. There were all kinds of things for sale at the "suqs" (small shop in Arabic) in Aswan – miniature gilt-covered Tutankhamuns, models of the pyramids, alabaster carvings, porcelain jars of all sizes, clay pottery, silver lockets of Nefertiti, the Ankh, gold, silver and metal bracelets, cartouches, galabiyas, figures of Horus and Anubis, scarab beetles, key chains, magnets, papyrus paintings, bookmarks, plates, and even tiny sarcophagi with the most horrendous-looking mummies inside them. My son was fascinated and wanted all of them – especially the sarcophagus with the mummy inside.

When you are on vacation, the spend-drive goes over-board and the purse strings loosen automatically. At least it is so for me.

I relented and bought my son a few knick-knacks that he wanted. And then I asked my daughter what she liked.

My daughter wanted none of anything we saw. Like all girls her age, all she wanted was a doll. I refused to buy her an Egyptian Barbie; we had nine of them at home, all gifted – none bought by me as I am not particularly fond of Barbie dolls – in various stages of undress. Their plastic breasts, pencil-thin waists and elongated curved heels, just do not agree with my sense of aesthetics or biology. Fortunately, it was easy to distract her and I managed to make her believe that she didn't want an Egyptian Barbie dressed in a *burkha*. So that made it easy to turn away from them.

We walked on and came across a supermarket which we decided to explore. My daughter came across two furry, cuddly toy cats in a tiny basket.

"Look Mummy. They are so cute!" she exclaimed "Pleeeeeeaase, can you buy it for me?"

My adult mind made a quick comparison of the price of the doll – about 55 Egyptian pounds; and the price of these cats – about 15 Egyptian pounds, and quickly found a clever solution. After all, most seasoned mothers know that the fascination with any toy, no matter how expensive, lasts precisely for three hours or till you reach home, whichever is earlier.

So I made a deal with her.

'If I buy you these cats, you cannot ask for a doll. Agreed?'

'Yes, Mummy. Thank you, Mummy. You are the best.' (*Preeti's Law of Parenting*: Amount of flattery and good manners is directly proportional to accession of demand.)

Then I took the cats in my hand to examine them – and jumped out of my skin in fright.

'*Miaow… Miaow… Miaow… I love you.*' They shrieked in unison. They screamed. I almost punctured an ear-drum. Their decibel level belied their cuteness and size.

'Wow Mummy, they can talk too!' My daughter's eyes were now shining with joy and anticipation.

The mewing was realistic and sounded exactly like real cats, except of course the 'I love you' bit. I turned it around. The label said: 'Made in China.'

'Baby, this is made in China,' I said.

'So what?' she asked indignantly.

'We are in Egypt, right? Don't you want something Egyptian?'

She looked at me like I was an idiot who didn't comprehend the simplest of things.

Then she said, 'Look Ma. We don't have to spend money to go to China to buy this. We are getting it here in Egypt. Isn't that great?'

You cannot fault logic like that. It was great. Besides, it was a thousand times better than the Barbies – with or without the burkhas. So I bought it.

We discovered another thing after we brought the cats back to India. We didn't have to touch the toy to make them talk. The slightest of vibrations was enough to set them off.

When the house-help was dusting the room, the Egyptian cats decided to give her a piece of their mind, or voice, to be precise.

She ran out of the room screaming: 'Didi – wahan billi hai. Usne baccha dala hai.' (There's a cat in the room and has given birth to kittens.) I had to show her the toy to convince her otherwise.

My mother who was visiting us woke up with a start in the middle of the night when the cats meowed and announced that they love her. She promptly threw them out of the room.

Those days I had to wake up at the unearthly hour of 5:30 am as my son had to be at school at 7:00 am. To make his lunch, I needed to be awake first, which meant coffee. I was making myself a cup and trying to simultaneously get the vessels out to cook his lunch.

In the half asleep, half-dazed, barely-there, groggy-eyed, fuzzy-brained state, I dropped the lid of the pan and it went crashing to the floor loudly.

'*Miaow... Miaow... Miaow... I love you.*' was the response.

I smiled. It is not every day that someone (or something) says they love you, early in the morning for dropping the lid of a vessel with a big clang.

Later, when I was unpacking from the Egypt trip, I realised that I hadn't bought any souvenir for myself. All I had was a nice pair of Lycra tights which I had purchased there.

I looked closely at the label. They were made in China as well.

A little love-note

Most people who don't have children, lead adult lives. They have a fairly stable routine and perhaps go out, catch a play or a movie during weekends, or go to a pub, or entertain themselves in a very adult fashion. The rest of us, parents, have our children.

Those who have children will agree with me when I say that each day there is a new drama which unfolds. You really don't need reality TV (move over *Big Boss*) when you have children. There is enough entertainment provided on a daily basis, except that sometimes you are an active participant, and at times, unwittingly the clown in this reality show. You don't even realise it till you put your feet up at the end of the day.

When my children were the school-going age, the best part of my day was when they came back from school. Each day when my two returned, I was there to greet them. I would usually make a nice snack, like *aloo-tikkis*, which they would gobble in a jiffy, showering me with ample amounts of "mmmmm... mummy, you are the best cook in the world". Once their little tummies were full, they would be gently cajoled to change out of their school uniforms after which they would cuddle up to me and tell me about their day. I loved listening to them. Each day, there was something new.

On most days, it would be my daughter who had a lot to narrate and my son would be a silent spectator.

But one day, my son, who was twelve at that time, had a story to share.

He said, 'Mum, today a boy in the school bus gave a note to a girl.'

'Ooh,' I said. This was interesting. From being a child, they were now slowly wading into the territory of being teens, having crushes and such things.

'Did you see what was in the note? Did he show it to you?' I asked.

'I could just see it from outside. He had folded it. He had written "from" and "to". That was all that was visible from the outside.'

'Oh,' I said, a bit disappointed to not know what was in the note. I thought it would be a juicy story.

But it was not over yet.

'Mum, the girl took it from him and said *aww* and she smiled,' continued my son.

'And?' I prompted him, now fully engrossed in his tale.

'Ma, when she opened it, there was a dead bee inside. She screamed her head off and then she threw it out of the window.'

I collapsed on the floor with laughter, my son and daughter joined in too.

A great way as any, to get the attention of your potential crush. Just gift them dead bees, and make them scream. They are sure to remember you.

A lot of times, it also seems like we are transported back to our childhood, through our children. The kids these days might be natives to the internet, might have had far more exposure than we did at their age, and might be tech-savvy little geniuses. But the fact is that children always are children, be it in today's world or be it a hundred years ago. The toys they play with might have changed, but the qualities inherent in children – a curious nature, a playful attitude, and most importantly, being unafraid to try out new things, unafraid to fail and the ability to quickly forgive and not carry grudges – still remain the same. We adults would do well to emulate some of these qualities.

The commando tooth fairy

We were living in the UK and the children were eight and five. They had their own rooms, and usually slept in their own beds. However, if one of them had a nightmare, we would find them wedged in between us. They would crawl into our bed in the middle of the night, and make themselves comfortable, under our duvet.

One night I was working late. When I went to my bedroom, I found my daughter fast asleep, next to my husband. She was unwell and was wheezing. I had given her medication and she seemed to be in deep sleep. I was too weary to move her. So I went to her room and slept in her bed.

My husband and I had forgotten that she had lost a tooth that day. She had carefully wrapped it in a tissue, labelled it "Tooth" and had slid it under the pillow, in my bed.

The next morning, my husband and I were woken up by indignant screams and foot-stomping by my daughter, who seemed miraculously fine. She was very upset that the tooth fairy had forgotten to give her money.

My husband and I looked at each other guiltily. The last time she lost a tooth, the tooth fairy had been very generous and given her five pounds. My son had proclaimed that the tooth fairy was biased since when he had lost his teeth back in India, the tooth fairy had paid him in Indian rupees. But when his sister lost her teeth, she was paying in Pound Sterling!

There was no time for arguments. So I tried pacifying her.

'Maybe the tooth fairy has to come from India and her flight is late,' I said.

She wasn't buying that.

'No, the tooth fairy has wings and she comes from the Tower of London," said my daughter with great certainty.

'Preeti, can you get my phone charger. It is in *your bag*,' said my husband.

Of course, I knew that his phone charger wasn't in my bag at all. The way he said "your bag" and the way he looked at me conveyed it all. We hadn't been married for fourteen years for nothing!

I frantically began searching for my bag which I remembered was downstairs, having been deposited dutifully on the sofa, after we got back from a weekend outing.

'Look carefully,' said my husband to my daughter. 'Maybe the tooth fairy left it there, and it has disappeared under the pillow.'

This convinced my daughter and she began looking very carefully all over my bed, for the money which the tooth fairy might have left.

It bought me enough time and I felt a bit like those commandos you see in war movies, who move from trench to trench, as I crept downstairs on all fours, retrieved my wallet from my handbag, and crawled back upstairs in a silent and stealthy manner. I did not even let out a whimper, though I did grimace in pain, when my bare knees got poked by a coin from the battleship game that had been left on the stairs. I was a true commando in action.

'Papa, there is no money anywhere here. I have looked everywhere,' said my daughter looking very disappointed.

'Ooooh. Maybe the tooth fairy got confused because you changed beds. Have you looked under *your* pillow in *your* bed?' asked my husband. The look that I had given him had conveyed what I wanted to say: that the mission was successful. He understood what I meant by that look.

My daughter rushed to her room, and looked under her pillow.

'Papa, mama! Look, the tooth fairy did leave me money under *my* pillow,' she beamed as she held up five shiny one pound coins.

'See, you changed rooms and the tooth fairy got confused. How was she to know that you weren't sleeping in your room?' I said.

'I am soooo happy, Mummy,' said my daughter. 'The tooth fairy not only gave me money, she also forgot to take my tooth. Now I can have my tooth *and* the money too!' She was delightedly dancing around.

What could I say? I just smiled and hugged her.

Most of the time, tooth fairies have to be very nimble-footed so that the children don't discover them. But sometimes, they also have to do the commando crawl and sleep in a different bedroom at night.

LOVE A LITTLE STRONGER

"I have found that if you love life, life will love you back."

– Arthur Rubinstein

The magic of faith

It was my daughter's Sports Day at school. She was six. It's a lovely age for the children to be, from a mother's point of view. Oh, the freedom that comes, when your infants finally cross that milestone of being toddlers, and are now mini-adults. For mothers, it means you don't have to change their diapers. They can converse with you, unlike the baby-babble of the past few years. They can tell you what they want, but most of all, they listen to you, adore you and think you are the most beautiful person on earth. Also, they want to be just like you when they grow up.

It was a hot summer day in India. The temperatures were soaring and the forecasts predicted that they would touch 40 degree Celsius, which is about 104 Fahrenheit.

Everyone who has gone to school in India knows how important the schools think "Sports Day practice" is. They make you rehearse drills, sometimes with ridiculous props such as painted coconut shells. I had that one time, when I was a student.

My daughter was a part of one such drill. She would have to be standing in the tropical mid-day sun for her sports day drill. She wanted to wear a cap. The school she went to has a prescribed cap. They have prescribed everything, right from school bags to watches to lunch bags to shoes to hair bands to even bloomers, all of which have to be bought at the school tuck shop. You cannot wear anything you like. It has to be the prescribed one. I hadn't bothered to buy a school cap till now. Now that she wanted it, I drove her to school that morning, so that I could buy the cap for her.

Throughout the journey to school, she kept chattering, excited about her Sports Day. She told me that I was the 'sweetest mother on earth' for agreeing to come to the tuck shop just to buy her a cap.

She is a sweet talker and her eyes shine with honesty, earnestness and enthusiasm. She hasn't learnt to lie. (Yet!)

When we reached the tuck shop, we were in for a disappointment.

They apologised, for the cap was out of stock. There were many other parents who had come to buy caps but had to return disappointed.

My daughter's face fell. She was looking forward to the cap that would shield her from the blazing sun.

She looked at me and asked, 'Now, what do we do, Mummy? It will be so hot and for three hours I have to stand in the sun.' (I don't know to this day if three hours was a figment of her imagination, but even fifteen minutes is bad enough during summers in India.)

I didn't know what to tell her.

'Don't worry,' I said, 'Today I'll tell the sun not to shine so hard.'

'Can you do that? Will he listen to you?'

'Of course, he will. Have you ever seen anyone not listening to your mother?'

She smiled and happily waved.

When she came back in the evening, she gave me a big hug.

'Mummy,' she said, 'the sun really listened to you. It wasn't so hot, mummy. You are the greatest.'

I hugged her back.

And just for that moment, I wanted to be six again.

A stranger's act of kindness

When my children were little, summer vacations were always spent in Kerala, in a tiny village which was where my parents lived. To my city-raised children, it was a magical world. They had never seen water being drawn from a well using a large iron bucket, which was lowered into the well with the help of a rope and a pulley. They had never held a pair of bunny rabbits in their hands. They had never climbed trees and plucked mangoes. So Kerala was always a big adventure for them.

All the folks in my parents' neighbourhood are very friendly. They speak only Malayalam and do not understand any other language. So my children who were fluent only in their mother tongue, Konkani, and English, were a bit of a novelty. They made friends with the local children and it was wonderful to see how they communicated and played with each other despite the language barrier.

The areas surrounding my parents' village as well — their quaint cottage, surrounded by a garden tended to lovingly by my mother, the rubber trees which formed a forest, a twenty-feet deep canal, little hills, trees full of ripening jackfruits and guavas, tiny shops that sold trinkets and other essentials, small bakeries, tea-shops — all of these were a novelty for my children. Life here is unhurried, leisurely, sleepy and peaceful.

One afternoon, we were taking a walk through the lush green paddy fields. Suddenly my children spotted two baby goats frolicking about. They were jumping from side to side and were very fast. The paddy field was the size of about three football fields. We stood there for a while mesmerised by their antics.

My daughter who was about six at that time, suddenly said, 'Mama, they are so cute, I wish I could hold them. I very badly want to.'

So I told her we could try, but the moment we got near them, they bounded away in no time, and were almost at the other end of the field.

Suddenly, a man emerged. He had been watching us, the "city dwellers", with amusement. He was bare-chested, dressed in traditional clothes, a *lungi*. He was pleased that I could speak Malayalam. He said the goat kids belonged to him and his children too loved to pet them. That was the reason he had bought them. He asked if my children would like to hold them. I told him they would be delighted, as these are things we do not get to do in the city.

He then chased the goat kids around the paddy field. It wasn't an easy task and in an expert manner, he managed to catch them. He then gave one to my son and one to my daughter. To say my children were overjoyed is to put it mildly. My children held them like treasures for a very long time. They petted them, played with them and the goat kids too, looked comfortable with them. It was an invaluable experience.

He was a complete stranger. I do not even know his name. Yet his face, and more importantly, the trouble he took to chase the baby goats around the field just for my children, is something that I remember to this day.

We left the paddy field with a happy-warm feeling and memories to last a lifetime. All because a complete stranger chose to do a random act of kindness, just to make two children happy.

Siblings without rivalry

My daughter was six and she reminded me a lot of Hermione Granger. She was a stickler for rules, almost always at the top of her class, bright, smart and like Hermione, if it was in a book, you could be sure that she had learnt it. She was, in other words, a teacher's dream student. She rarely forgot to take anything that the teacher had said must be brought to class, even if the teacher herself had forgotten!

The school my children went to at that time was a very strict school. Apart from being a stickler for rules, the other thing they insisted upon was the dress code. There was simply no room for deviating from the prescribed uniforms. They had two sets of uniforms – the summer wear and winter wear. The winter uniform had the tie, the blazer, the school belt and school ID card that each child had to compulsorily wear. In addition, the girls had to wear a dark green hair band and dark green rubber bands for ponytails as well. If any child was seen without any of the above-mentioned accessories, they were labelled "defaulters" and were punished.

That day, long after the children had left for school, I discovered to my horror, that my daughter had forgotten to wear her blazer. The school did not allow parents inside the school premises once the assembly bell had rung. So there was no way I could reach it to her. I felt bad when I discovered it, as it meant she would be punished, more so since she had a special assembly that day.

Being punished and being pulled up at school was the ultimate disaster, a "loss of face" and end of the world, in her book. She would not be able to take it lightly.

There was nothing I could do but wait for the children to come back from school. I was certain there would be huge tears rolling down her face when she came home, and that I would have to comfort her and hug her. I prepared myself mentally, to spend the rest of my evening consoling her.

I was wrong. They came back from school, my daughter with a big smile on her face and wearing an over-sized blazer – her brother's! I was dumbstruck. After they boarded the bus to go to school, my son who was ten at the time, realised that she would get punished. He took off his blazer and made her wear it. She was not caught. He was. He said he was a defaulter and owned up. I wondered what must have gone through his mind when he did that. I was so proud of him for protecting his younger sister. I was moved too, by his selfless act.

On some days, when they fought, it looked as though they hated each other and would kill each other if allowed to. Those were the days I wondered where I went wrong in raising them.

But the day my son did this was one of those days, when I went to bed with a happy-warm feeling, knowing that I must be doing something right, after all.

When adversity strikes

A long time ago, there was a grumpy old man who lived in my neighbourhood. I had never seen him smile. I don't think anyone could have claimed that they had either. He used to saunter around the whole residential complex, like a displeased dictator surveying his province. He looked angry, irritated and ready to bite off your head, if you dared so much as meet his eye. I had never seen anyone greeting him or talking to him.

When I had first moved into this neighbourhood, I had tried to strike up a conversation with him. My enthusiastic greetings of "Good morning" or "Good evening" were met with a curt nod of the head. It was saying, 'How dare you break this invisible wall of "Leave me alone" that I had created around myself?' I persisted for about a month or so. After that, I gave up. I continued to greet him though, when eye-contact was unavoidable. But most of the time, I turned the other way. I did not need a grouch spoiling my day.

The old man lived with his wife, son, daughter-in-law and their two children. One day, his wife invited us for a cup of tea. I dreaded accepting the invitation as I had no interest in making conversation with the grumpy old man. But she was very persistent. It would have been churlish to not accept, and so I finally did. I did not want to meet the old man or talk to him.

To my surprise, he wasn't around.

The old man's wife got talking to me. She was jovial and her personality was a direct contrast to that of her husband's. She was helpful, kind and courteous. She also talked a lot. Perhaps she was lonely or perhaps she found me to be a good listener.

She told me about their life before they had moved to this place. She seemed happy to talk and she told me a lot of things. She told me they had lost an adult son who had been mentally challenged. They had spent years caring for him, taking him to a special school, bringing him back, looking after him. She knew a lot about caring for people with special needs.

Sometimes, when my two normal, healthy children fight, do not listen to me and drive me up the wall, I feel angry like all parents, and lose my cool. I wondered how this couple coped with caring for a fully grown adult who could not do anything for himself, as also another child with normal needs. I felt her pain as she spoke about the long years that had gone into caring for her adult son. To get away from the memories, they had sold their house and moved here, after he had died.

For the first time, I began realising what a big burden the old man must have carried in his younger years. No wonder he was this way. Perhaps the years had taken their toll on him. But the very next instant, I couldn't help reflecting that his wife too had gone through the same thing. He was working and she had been the primary care-giver. To that extent, it was logical that she should have been more affected than him. Yet, her attitude to life was completely different from his.

It reminded me of the egg, carrot and coffee bean story, which I had read, and which has recently been doing the rounds on social media as a video. When a young daughter complained about how hard her life was and how she had many problems, her mother took her to the kitchen and handed her an egg, a carrot and a coffee bean. She placed three boiling pots of water on the stove and asked her daughter to drop the egg, the carrot and the coffee bean into each of them.

After about fifteen minutes of boiling, the carrot, which was hard to begin with, came out soft and squishy. The egg, fragile to begin with, became hard-boiled. It was only the ground coffee bean which was unique. It retained its original form, yet gave out something useful – coffee. It didn't itself change, but it changed the water it had been dropped into. The mother asked the daughter which one she would like to be when adversity struck – a carrot, an egg or a coffee bean.

That evening when I came home, I thought about the old man and his wife for a long time. She was indeed a coffee bean. I looked at the old man too, differently. He couldn't help being what he was – an egg. I made a mental note to resume greeting him every day.

A promise

Death is something that terrifies everyone. Its harshness and finality is hard to accept. Most of us pretend it does not exist and most of us dislike talking about it. Many parents tell their children that loved ones who have passed away become "stars" or "angels" and that they watch over us.

When someone dear to us dies, the feeling of loss stays with us. We carry the pain in our hearts. We learn to cope. We learn to manage without them. We remember what our loved ones used to say and we try our best to recall every detail about them, so that we keep them alive in our memories.

My children had to face the death of my father at a very early age. My son was eight and my daughter was five, when my father who they were very close to, died all of a sudden.

My dad as a grandfather, was every child's dream come true. He was very close to all of us, and especially to my children. My children fondly recall the games that my dad had taught them. My parents lived in a tiny village in Kerala, right next to thousands of rubber tree plantations. Like all small villages there, it is lush green, verdant, peaceful and the pace of life is leisurely, slow and unhurried. It is nature at its best. It is picture-perfect.

Any visit to their grandparents' home meant hours of endless fun, climbing trees, walking through paddy fields, petting baby goats, eating guavas picked off trees and swimming in the river with my dad. My children were devastated when he died all of a sudden, without any warning or even a hint of things to come. He died in the middle of a conversation with mom. Just like that. One moment he and mom were watching their favourite show on TV and the next moment he was gone. My mom had initially thought that he had fallen asleep, unusual though it was. In a way, he had. Except that from this one, there was no waking up. It was a massive cardiac arrest.

My children then knew that death could creep in that way too.

We were living in the UK at that time, and often, my son and I used to talk, long after my daughter had drifted off to sleep, after their bedtime reading ritual. I don't know if it was the quietness of the night or the intimacy of being cosily curled up in a warm bed, hugging me, that reassured him – he loved this talk time. We discussed many things each night. He told me what he was thinking and I mostly listened. He would weigh his thoughts against my inputs and draw his own conclusions.

One night, the gravity of the conversation brought a lump to my throat.

'Mummy, how do you think I will die?'

'Hmm, I wish I could answer that but I don't know, son.'

I hugged him tighter.

'I wish God made a world where nobody is born and nobody dies and things just stay the same.'

'I wish that too. I wish I could just freeze this moment in time. You will still be eight forever and I won't grow any older.'

'No, Mummy. I wouldn't want that. Then I'd have to go to school forever! Who wants to do that? I want to grow up soon, buy a car and take you around.'

'Make that a Ferrari. I love Ferraris!' He was quiet for a minute. Then he whispered, 'I would hate to die without you Mummy.' I didn't know what to say. So I was silent.

'Do you promise that you won't die before me?' he asked, looking at me earnestly, his eyes shining in the dark, his tiny hands clutching mine.

'I promise.'

'Promises should never be broken,' my dad used to always say. I always try to keep mine. But today, I made one that I hope I never have to keep.

We lay in silence after that, each of us lost in our own thoughts. And that night, I held him long after he drifted off to sleep.

BE THE BEST YOU CAN BE

"At the core of your heart, you are perfect and pure. No one and nothing can alter that."

— Amit Ray

"Believe it can be done. When you believe something can be done, really believe, your mind will find the ways to do it. Believing a solution paves the way to solution."

— David J. Schwartz

Please hug me – I'm just like you

This incident happened more than a decade ago. Yet it gives me goose bumps each time I think about it. It was a soul-stirring, heart-wrenching experience. It moved me and humbled me so completely. I still haven't recovered. I don't think a lifetime is enough.

I happened to be there just because of my circumstances at that time. We were based in Pune and my husband's organisation had their Corporate Social Responsibility activities planned, throughout the year, where employees could choose which weekends they would like to take up, for fulfilling these.

That particular weekend, they were short of volunteers and so I offered to go with the team to Manavya. I had never heard of them until then. Manavya is one of the few non-government organisations in India that offers residential care and rehabilitation to HIV/AIDS affected destitute/orphaned children and women.

Its mission is to enable children and women living with HIV, to get a fair fighting chance to survive and overcome odds; to ensure their rights to food, clothing, health, shelter and education without social discrimination.

I was told that there weren't many people who were willing to go there and spend time with the children. It may be because, despite us knowing that we will not contract AIDS by touching someone, we still have that mental fear and loathing for the disease. It reminded me of Tom Hanks in *Philadelphia*.

There were just three of us that day. The other two had no previous experience with children. During those days, I used to do thinking workshops for kids in international and alternate schools. So, of the three, I was the most experienced.

We were all a bit nervous. This was the first time that any of us were doing anything like this. We had heard that these kids were those abandoned by society and nobody visited them much. Therefore, when someone did, they would hug you and there would be a lot of physical display of affection. Mostly to ease our nervousness, and also because the drive was very long, we got talking. One of them extolled the virtues of an expensive boarding school. He had been to one, and he tried to convince me of the advantages of sending one's children to such a school. I heard him out patiently but did not see any point in offering my views, as the debate on "boarding school versus day school" is endless.

When we reached, we were welcomed by the folks who ran the place, and we were given a small briefing about the organisation and its mission. We learnt that there were about sixty children, all of them HIV positive and many with full blown AIDS. Some, with just a few days to live. They thanked us for taking out time for them.

We were led to a large hall, from which there was happy laughter emanating. When I actually saw the children, the first thing that struck me was, that I had been nervous for no reason. They were just a bunch of kids, like any other that I had handled. This just seemed like a regular bunch of kids.

It was then that I saw their purple mouths. Almost all of them had a kind of tincture rubbed around their mouths. I later learnt that it was to prevent infections. They were not conscious of it at all. They smiled and laughed, and were waiting for me to take over. I taught them a little dance and a funny song. I talked to them. They hugged me and I hugged them back. I listened to them and made them laugh. After that, it was time for Art. They were to make pictures – anything that they felt like drawing. Many drew happy pictures. There were very few who knew their full names. All these children were abandoned children of commercial sex workers. The ones who knew their full names wrote it proudly. Usually, most children relate to me and open up to me. But there was one child to whom I could not get through, no matter how hard I tried. I tried to make him laugh. He did not even smile. His picture was a scribble of just one colour. Black.

Later, we distributed gifts and chocolates. What was most unusual was that there was no grabbing or asking or pushing. The children were very polite. They took it and said "thank you". One could almost sense a calm acceptance in them, like the limited number of days many of them had. Two of them said that they wanted an extra one, not for themselves, but for their friends who were too sick to come for the session. I went inside and saw them. They were tucked into their beds. Beside them were the sweets and the gifts which we had earlier distributed. These children were really used to looking out for one another and looking after each other.

The afternoon turned into dusk and we said our goodbyes. How trivial all our problems seemed compared to the ones these children faced every day.

We came back in taciturn silence. There was nothing to talk about.

The little black dot

Many years back, something that a teacher said made a deep impact and has remained with me though all these years. It was my Math teacher, whom I liked a lot, and this must have been in Class 7 or so. She came in one day, all charged and excited. We had a white board those days, apart from the regular black board. The white board was used for "important things". That day, she had a black marker in her hand, which meant she was using the white board. That by itself made all of us sit still and pay attention.

She drew a dot with the black marker in the centre of the board.

'What do you all see?' she asked.

We looked at the board. It was nothing but a black dot. We all said that we saw a black dot.

'Does anybody see anything other than a black dot?' she asked. Nobody did.

Then she said, 'In life, people look only at that small black dot. There might be a vast expanse of white. But if there is a tiny black dot, your focus is going to be on that. We forget to look at the big picture. We focus on that little, small, insignificant dot that really is minuscule, in the large scheme of things – and we forget about the white that exists.'

It made profound sense back then. It still does, more than two decades later. It is something that has helped me sail through the many adversities that life threw on my path.

One time, when my children were little, both were down with a viral fever, and my husband was travelling. Both were burning hot and wanted to hug me all the time. It is exhausting looking after two children when they are healthy itself – so when they are sick, single parenting can be really very gruelling. And that is putting it mildly. Anybody who has gone through this will tell you how hard it is, to manage on your own with no help whatsoever from parents or in-laws. We have always been a nuclear family and so when one of us travels on work, the other handles the home and the children.

That morning was particularly bad. Not only were the children ill, but it looked like I too was coming down with something. As though that was not enough, the house-help decided to go AWOL. I was going through a down-in-the-dumps-how-will-I-manage-this-is-so-tough kind of a phase till I chatted with a good friend. Something she said made me guffaw. Things at once began looking better. Whoever said that laughter is the best medicine indeed had got it absolutely right.

Later, I remembered the black dot theory. Most of us focus on that black dot. In relationships, in situations, in people, our attention is invariably drawn to that little black dot. Most of the time we do forget the big white expanse that is waiting for us to fill it with bright colours, with happy memories, with laughter. This is possible only if you let go of that little black dot, or integrate it deftly and quickly with the big picture.

Black dots, just like morose, sad and grumpy people, will always exist. It is how you handle them that matters. And if you have a friend who helps you look at the big picture – hold on to that friendship for life. Do not focus on the little black dots that may crop up in it at some point of time. Do *everything* you can to keep your friendship going.

True friendship is indeed priceless.

The two forces

We used to live in the UK for a while, in a small quiet town with acres and acres of splendid parks, lush greenery, picturesque, calm and serene. It felt like I was living inside a painting or a picture postcard.

I would many a time, sit and watch my children as they played in the park. Having earlier worked with children, I couldn't help observing that children are exactly the same across cultures, the world over. They are open-minded, curious, frank, honest and most importantly, they are unafraid to make mistakes.

Those children that day were talking and discussing what they would become when they grew up. It was a serious discussion and they meant every word of it, with complete conviction and zero doubt. One was sure he wanted to be superman. Another said that he wanted to work at a pizza store. A third said he wanted to fly a plane. A little girl said she wanted to work in a big office, just like her mother. Another wanted to be a hair-stylist.

It made me think how different they are from adults. They are not afraid to imagine and they are not afraid to share their dreams. They are not afraid to fall down and if they do, they just get up and carry on with life. It made me wonder why we adults do not have the enthusiasm that children do, to try out new things. Why are we so enclosed in our comfort zones, so reluctant to step out?

I think there are many reasons for it. The simplest way to make sense of it would be to accept that within each of us, are two forces that are constantly at work, at any given point in our lives.

Most of us are pulled apart by two opposing force – Mr Yes and Mr No. You can call them Ms Yes and Ms No, if you prefer. Or just Y and N, to keep it really simple

Y likes you. Y appreciates anything you do. When you look in the mirror Y says, 'Yes, you look good. You aren't fat. You have not put on weight. Your complexion is looking clearer. You are smart. Yes, I like you. You are great, gorgeous, the best person in the world. I like hanging around with you and you make me happy. You are talented, smart and witty. The people in your life value you and you are important to them.'

N is cruel, a sadist who delights in your discomfort. N criticises anything you do. 'You can be thinner. You look tired. What are those dark circles under your eyes? You are just average. I am not too fond of you. What you are doing is nothing great. You are unsuccessful. You are unimportant. You are foolish, silly and unattractive.'

Y believes in you. Y thinks you can achieve anything. N tells you that your ideas are not good. N reminds you what it is to be ridiculed. Y sets you free. N holds you back.

N is rarely useful. N might help you make that effort to push yourself a little more, as N convinces you that you aren't good enough. But if you let N take over completely, you get defeated. However, if you let Y take over completely, you would be deluding yourself. I think there probably is a middle path between N and Y, which we have to try and walk on. This balancing act is hard. I tend to lean more towards Y, simply because you end up being a more optimistic and nicer person to be around. Also, you feel good about yourself.

Psychologists agree that it is because of N that many people find it difficult to accept or give praise. When you praise someone sincerely, instead of accepting it as a compliment and saying thank you, they dismiss it as flattery. Or they look for insincerity where there is none. When genuine compliments that you pay are hurled back at you, it is akin to giving a person a gift, and having them throw it back on your face.

N does not let you believe in goodness – be it in yourself or in others. Many people find it difficult to tell others that they really admire them, or give praise for something they did. You see, it is N at work. 'What will that person think? Will she/he think that I want something and so I am praising them? How will I sound?'

When we try to step out of our comfort zones, there is a constant battle going on inside most of us, between starry-eyed affirmation and disapproving negation.

When I was thinking of writing this book, N tried to stop me. Actually, there was N and many other people in the voice of N. I am glad Y managed to defeat them.

If N pops up when you really want to pursue your dreams, it is best to tell N to vamoose. Shoo N away. Squish N. Do not let N anywhere in. Keep N out.

This simple philosophy has been propounded by many positive thinkers and is described in several books. Paulo Coelho, Rhonda Byrne, Robin Sharma, Norman Vincent Peale – all of them convey a similar underlying message. They believe that people can shape their thoughts and use the laws of attraction to turn their lives around. What most of them say is that you should deeply and badly want it from the heart (not merely an unexpressed wishful thinking).

Powerful words indeed: 'Believe and you shall achieve.'

Keeping a journal

Ever since I can remember, I have had a journal. I think I first started writing in a journal when I was seven or probably eight. I did not know then why I wanted to keep one, especially since the danger of it being discovered by the other family members was great. I only knew that the world made much more sense once I finished penning my thoughts down. My journal was a way of slowing down, of processing the information rushing through my brain, and thinking through, and deciding the best course of action. More than anything, my journal gave me power over my feelings, my thoughts and my life. It helped me plan out my future course of action.

Today, most successful people advocate keeping a journal. One of the books that I read, a wonderful book by Julia Cameron called *The Artist's Way,* had these lines, which spoke to me:

"In times of pain, when the future is too terrifying to contemplate and the past too painful to remember, I have learned to pay attention to right now. The precise moment I was in was always the only safe place for me."

So **why** should you keep a journal? How will it help you?

1. **A record of now:** Keeping a journal is a record of your now. Your present reality. Your goals. Your dreams. Your aspirations. It

is important to record them, as they are fleeting, momentary. They can deceive you. But once you capture them in your journal, they act as a constant reminder for you to aspire for change – and that is so important to grow.

2. **Slotting time:** Without a journal, one day merges into another, merges into a third. Time is a blur. With a journal, there is a goal, a map, a "place to go".
   It is a blueprint to shape your life.

3. **It is fun:** If you feel writing a journal is monotonous, you can make a bullet journal. Or a scrapbook of "wishes". Make it fun. Make it any way you want. There are no hard and fast rules. But do maintain one.

4. **Record of growth:** You will see how much you have grown from the time you start it, to a few years then on.

5. **Clearer thought process:** When you start writing in a journal, your thought process becomes clearer. You tend to start becoming more assertive. Your dreams materialise.

I have kept a journal ever since I was a child. I don't write every day, but I do write regularly. From 2005 onwards, I stopped keeping chronological diaries. Instead, I write when I feel like writing, and I put the date.

Try it.

Read up about the different journals that you can keep.

Then start one, and see where it takes you.

I can say one thing with certainty – you will only have a lot to gain.

Resolutions

At the end of each year, many people all around the world make their new year resolutions. Some break it just after a week. Some stick to it for as long as three months. And some really determined souls actually succeed in carrying them out.

I like making resolutions, as it feels to me like a fresh start. You could technically make resolutions on any day of the year. Each day is as good as any to make a new beginning. But somehow, there is something special about a new year – it holds the promise of possibilities. One year, on New Year's eve, as I was sitting down to make my resolution, I just could not help thinking that as each day passes, we are one day closer to our death.

Juxtaposed against this realisation, my new year resolutions, which until all these years dealt with the mundane and minutiae of daily life, suddenly took the form of urgency. I decided I would make a list that everybody *can* follow. In fact, not sticking to it would be difficult!

When my friends read it, they endorsed it whole-heartedly. Many even took printouts of this list and stuck it on their cupboards.

Here is what **was** on my list:

1. *Laugh heartily:* Wikipedia defines laughter as "an audible expression or appearance of merriment or amusement or an inward feeling of joy and pleasure". Science has proven that laughter strengthens our immune system, helps us fight illnesses and reduces problems associated with diseases such as high blood pressure, strokes, arthritis and ulcers.

   There are more than six thousand laughter yoga clubs in sixty countries.

   Some of these laughter clubs that have sprouted across my neighbourhood first shocked me. Initially, I was startled by the noise. A group of people about forty in number, all gathered together and laughing like lunatics for no reason was a concept that I had never come across before. At first I thought it was thunder in the middle of the summer season and was puzzled. Later, when I watched them, I too laughed, because laughter is so infectious.

   Humans are the only animals in nature who can laugh. (What hyenas do is not real laughter.) Research shows that just a few generations ago, healthy humans spent twenty minutes a day or more in laughter. But in today's time, laughing time is down to less than five minutes a day in most countries. Everybody loves to have a good laugh. No wonder humour shows and stand-up comedians are flourishing on television shows. If you have a crazy pal who makes you go into peals of laughter, hold on to that friendship. Nurture it, cherish it. It is priceless.

2. *Spend time with children:* The US Department of Health and Human Services conducted a study which measured how people benefited when they spent half an hour or more with children. They suggested that if you do not have kids of your

own, volunteer at the local child centre or rely on nieces and nephews or children of friends. If you mingle with children, it will awaken the inner child in you. If you have your own kids, take time out every day and really pay attention to what they want. Many of us are so busy being parents (get up, brush your teeth, do your homework, hurry or you will be late) that we forget to be a friend. A friend of mine always says, 'Don't just present gifts to children. Be present as a gift to them.'

3. *Stay away from the grouches and the Drains:* I have written about Radiators and Drains. (See the chapter with the same title.) Move away from the Drains and seek out the Radiators who will bring sunshine into your lives.

4. *If you love someone, say it:* It is really important to say the words. If that is not possible, show it. An unexpected hug can say so much. Miss no opportunity to tell the people who matter that you really love them. If you are shy, send a text. Send an e-card. Send a real card – do whatever it takes, but express it. It will not only make you feel good about yourself, but it will thrill the person who is the object of your affection too. (Provided it is reciprocal love.) Nobody can predict what will happen in the next twenty-four hours. So while you feel it, express it. It may not last forever, but make the most of it while it does.

5. *Be content with your body:* As long as we are fit and healthy, we should be happy. After all, we aren't going to model for the *Playboy* centrefold, a muscle and fitness magazine, nor are we going to star in a porn movie. The media bombards us with images of men with six pack abs and impossibly thin women. A majority of us have skewed perceptions of an ideal body. This does not mean that one should not strive to lose weight. If one is reasonably fit, one should be happy. A friend was diagnosed with a terminal illness and was given about three months to

live. She had two children aged six and three. Another friend's husband who had a high flying career passed away at a young age because of a brain tumour, leaving behind his wife and two daughters. Nobody ever thought that something like that could happen to him.

I realised how thankful one has to be if one is healthy, when I was in the hospital with typhoid, fighting for my life. That was an eye-opening moment when I realised that even if one does not have a picture-perfect body, what really matters is to be blessed with the gift of health.

6. *Enjoy the small things:* Look at the sunrise. You are gifted one every single day. Look at the flowers – if there are no flowers, look at the greenery or the waves in the ocean or the blueness of the sky or the placid flowing of the river or the stillness of a lake or the flight of an eagle. Isn't nature marvellous? Take off on a hike. Camp outdoors. Reconnect with nature. One of my favourite activities continues to be lying in my hammock and gazing at the stars.

Whatever you choose to do – live, love and laugh.

White lies

Almost all of us are guilty of lying to ourselves. Why do we do it? Why do we fool ourselves?

We do it, because it is an easy way out. The hard-hitting truth is that most of us are lazy. We want the path of least resistance. We want things to happen easily. The second reason we do it is out of fear. Most of us are so afraid of change. We fear the unknown. We fear rejection. We fear failure.

Over the years, I have discovered that many a time, I too have been guilty of telling little white lies to myself – but that does not definitely make it okay! I am happier when I face the truth and take action on what I can act upon.

Here are seven white lies we all tell ourselves:

1. **If only _____ (fill in suitably) came back to my life, I would be happy:** After my books became bestsellers, hundreds of people have written to me lamenting over a love lost. Sometimes the person would have walked out. Sometimes they would have dumped somebody. They keep thinking that if things went back to what they used to be, they would be happier.

For me, I faced my biggest personal loss when I lost my father (who meant the world to me) all of a sudden in 2006. There had not been a single day when I would not have spoken to my father on the phone. He was hale, hearty, healthy. And then in a moment, he was no more. For nearly three years I was totally stricken by grief, so much that I felt debilitated. I kept thinking that if only dad was around, I would be happy.

Even to this day, I cannot deny that there are days when I miss him so much that it almost hurts physically, especially when I achieve success and he is not there to share it. But I also now recognise how my life has changed *because* he is no longer around and because I learnt to *take action,* and not keep lamenting.

2. **I would do it if only I had the time:** Many of us fool ourselves saying, 'I really want to do it, but I do not have the time.' That is a big lie. The truth is, time is just an excuse. If you want to do it that badly, you will always *find* the time or *make* the time. If it is that important to you, you will! You can cut out on your TV viewing time. (Personally I do not watch TV at all and I only watch movies and that too after reading up the ratings on IMDB.) Or perhaps the time you waste gabbing on the phone? (I do not know what works for you, but when I am writing, I do not answer the phone and I do not answer the doorbell too.) We can get up an hour earlier (yeah, it is okay to get just seven hours of sleep – you won't get any dark circles under your eyes!) if we desperately want to do something.

3. **It's okay to be a little bit overweight and to have a beer-belly or love handles, especially if you are married/ middle-aged/older:** It is definitely *not* okay! Personally, I know many people who are in their forties, fifties and even seventies who are in *terrific* shape. I know a seventy-year-old,

who could any day, give a twenty-five-year-old stiff competition in fitness. I truly want to be like him when (and if) I reach his age.

Being healthy and fit does work wonders when it comes to self-esteem (especially in the jealousy department). It is indeed important to work out and adopt a healthy lifestyle.

A friend of mine once told me, 'But you are married and a mother of two. You can afford to put on weight.' I could have murdered that friend. It is *awful* to let oneself go, just because one is married or has become a parent.

4. **I will get around to it someday, just as soon as _____ (fill in suitably):** This is another lie we tell ourselves. I am guilty of this too. Many a time, when I do not want to do something, I find that it is easier to just lie to myself saying I will eventually get around to it "someday". The "someday" never comes and suddenly one finds that *years* have gone by and now it is impossible to do it. Procrastination is indeed the biggest thief of Time. If you want to do it, do it today. Do it now! And no, it cannot wait! :)

5. **If only _____ had not happened, I would have been better off:** This is again a "wish it could have been" lament. I was guilty of this too. But then I realised that certain events happened and only because they happened did certain other events happen, and though it did cause me a lot of pain, it also helped me *grow* as a person. I learnt so much from it about myself, about people, about life. Today I am more accepting and less resentful about those things that happened which caused me so much grief, but which I could do nothing about but go with it.

6. **I have to do _____ (fill in suitably), else my partner will get mad at me:** This is probably a lie we so

cleverly believe that we might find it hard to even accept that we are lying. The fact is, we do have a choice. We have a choice to make our partner understand. But it involves confrontation and explaining. Most of us like to avoid that. I have broken off friendships (which caused me pain), simply because I felt too much pressure from the other end to conform to their ideal view of how I should be. I did try (a *lot*) to explain, to make the other person see it from my perspective. But I did not succeed. I am happier today because I have been true to myself.

Please realise that I am in no way advocating break-ups just because your partner does not see your point of view!! It would be really foolish to be so presumptive. But I do think that certain things, one *has* to stand up for, if it means a lot to you.

7. **I am not talented enough:** You are! All it takes is constant practice. Some might argue – how can it be, when they do not have even one artistic bone in their body? I would say to such people: that you have not found the right teacher. Yes, there is a difference between a natural gift and one that is cultivated. But it definitely *can* be cultivated. For example, I am not musical at all. (Satish is very musical and he has an ear for music. He sings well too and can pick up tunes on his own and play the keyboard and guitar.) But I did learn to play the keyboard and since I did not have a natural gift, I had to work doubly hard, but play it I did. The same goes for drawing portraits, playing a sport – anything really. You *can*, if you work hard enough!

So what lie are you going to stop telling yourself today?

DIY

When your life spirals out of control and you are utterly helpless to fix it, here are eight things that you *must* do, to feel instantly better.

1. **Focus on the things going right:** Often we forget about things that are going right for us. Do you have a roof over your head? Great! There are a 100 million homeless people worldwide. Do you have a job? Fabulous! There are more than 202 million unemployed people in the world. Often we take these things for granted. But if you really think about it, these are truly blessings, which are to be counted. If you have a job, and a home to live in, send out gratitude to the world.

2. **Refuse to talk or think about it**: If you have tried every possible thing that you can do, then put a *full stop* to your thoughts and to your mouth. Refuse to talk about it. The moment you find yourself cribbing to your spouse or friends or closest ones, the ones who are "duty-bound" or bound out of love to listen to how hard it is for you and how helpless you are, ask yourself to shut the f★★★ up. *Stop!* There is nothing more you can do.

3. **Exercise:** Why will exercise help when you have an issue in your hand that you can do nothing about? Well, exercise releases in your body, the feel-good endorphins. It fights depression. It makes you fitter. It helps you burn off that irresistible plum cake you gobbled. It also makes you so tired, so you don't toss and turn in bed, trying to fall asleep thinking about your problem. So put on your walking shoes, plug in your favourite podcast or music and hit the road. Go!

4. **Meet new people**: Go out and socialise. Get off the social media. Stop looking at other people's pictures and thinking about how great their lives are, while things are going so wrong with yours. Everybody is happy on Facebook. Go join a class which you have always wanted to attend. Go visit a friend you have been forever meaning to catch up with. If you have a chance to meet new people, grab it and do so. It will give you a different perspective about life, take your mind off the issue that you can do nothing about.

5. **Do something you have never done before:** When I found myself utterly helpless about a situation that I was facing one time, I joined Ashtanga Yoga. It is something I have never done before, even though I have practised yoga for more than thirty years. It gave me focus, concentration and turned me into the fittest version of myself that I have ever been in my life. I put all my energies into that and ignored the issue that I had no solution for, could do nothing about. I just took one day at a time and kept going till a solution emerged.

6. **Create something:** Think of something to do. Make something. If it has been long since you played with colours, go to the local art store, pick out some supplies and pour your feelings out in colour. You can paint as badly as you want. The

important thing is to just let yourself go free. Psychological research proves it.

7. **Clear your room:** If you can't muster the energy to clear the whole house, clean up your room. Get rid of all that you no longer need. Do what Marie Kondo tells you to! I have tried it. It works. It leaves you feeling lighter, more positive and happier.

8. **Give it time:** Please remember that no matter how much you try to "solve a problem", there is "a time" for it to be solved. There is sweet nothing you can do till the stars align. Sometimes, leaving a thing alone is the best solution.

10 things I learnt from my children

This was written on Mother's Day, many years back. Years later, these nuggets of wisdom still hold good, even in our adult lives. Here are ten things that I learnt from my children.

1. When someone smiles at you, see if the smile reaches their eyes. If only their lips smile and their eyes do not, then be very wary of them.
2. A tight hug topped with a kiss can solve most problems.
3. When you say "I love you", it helps if you say loooooooooooooooooove. :)
4. No matter how full you are, there is always room for a chocolate ice-cream.:)
5. "Just now" can stretch anywhere from two minutes to a couple of hours, depending on what activity has to be done.
6. If someone is angry with you, just hide under your bed till they cool down. But be sure that they don't find you there!
7. When you spill something, clean it up quickly if you do not want others to know about it.

8. It is sometimes okay to not tell the truth if it makes someone feel bad.
9. It is best not to lie, especially when you have not done your homework.
10. Some people might say they are your friend just because they want to play with your toys.

On Mother's Day, as I reflect, I am grateful I had the opportunity to be a mother to two wonderful children. It has truly taught me patience, kindness, understanding, perseverance and above all, the infinite power of love.

If you're fortunate to have a mother, be sure to call her and tell her what is going on in your life. It will make her very happy. You would be surprised how very little it takes to make mothers happy.

If you're a mother yourself, you know exactly what I am talking about.

Fifty-one things
and counting

I have been blogging for ten years now. That's a long time. There is so much that I have learnt and incorporated in my daily life.

1. You will never be able to please everybody.
2. You will have people who pull you down.
3. Ignore the snide remarks. Some people are like that.
4. The worst thing you can do to a person who enthusiastically shares something is being indifferent.
5. Negativity needs to be nipped in the bud.
6. Say a NO-ENTRY to the "wise" know-it-alls in your life.
7. If you feel drained each time you interact with them, they might be an energy vampire.
8. Seek out that which you love.
9. Do one happy thing every day.
10. Learn to ignore.
11. Don't waste time responding to trivial stuff on social media.
12. There will be down days.
13. There will be up days too.

14. People are mostly sweet, kind, warm and loving.
15. The world you see is a reflection of you.
16. You get what you send out.
17. You will always find your tribe.
18. Do your own thing.
19. Don't get involved in the drama in other people's lives.
20. Be consistent.
21. Mean what you say.
22. Love yourself.
23. Do one kind selfless deed for someone.
24. There's a 'block' feature on your messaging app. Use it!
25. It's very important to be grateful for the genuine people in your life.
26. Write every day. You need not publish it.
27. Treat yourself.
28. The world won't always be kind to you.
29. Some days will plain suck.
30. Invest in genuine friendships.
31. Even your closest friends will hurt you at some point of time.
32. Things change.
33. Ego is a powerful thing. Learn to keep it in check.
34. Be humble.
35. Don't think you are above everyone else.
36. BREATHE DEEPLY.
37. Let go.
38. The best is yet to come.
39. Life throws you curveballs. Learn to turn with the road.
40. Success is measured by the memories you leave behind.
41. The damp squibs probably need a healthy dose of sunshine.
42. You can do it!
43. You may feel hopeless right now, but the tide always changes.

44. Meet people face to face.
45. Spend time alone.
46. There are many "attention seekers". Ask if they deserve yours.
47. Your creative energy has to be harnessed.
48. Nourish your soul as well as your body.
49. Meditate.
50. READ.
51. And a last one: You can go on long after you think you can't.

Are you a Radiator or a Drain?

'Why is it that we hit it off instantly with some people whom we have just met, and with some, even when we have known them for years, we never really achieve that comfort?' asked my friend as she kicked off her footwear, tucked in her legs and sank back into the cane swing chair that she was sitting on.

We were having tea in her terrace garden, and enjoying the warm weather, just before the Indian summer set in. The beautiful flowers that were in bloom in her lush, landscaped space nodded in the breeze.

'I have experienced that too. Perhaps it is an energy match. Or a match of wave-lengths. We feel like we have known them forever, isn't it?' I said. I told her then about a lady whom I had met on a flight, who I instantly seemed to form a bond with. She told me her life story. And I listened. We exchanged phone numbers at the end of the flight – something I almost never do.

The lady said that she felt a deep connection with me. We felt happy in each other's company. It was strange. My friend understood. She said she had experienced that too. And she added that with some people, she felt an instant dislike, even though they might not even have said a word.

I told her then about what I had read somewhere a long time back. That people can be classified into Radiators and Drains.

'What? Radiators and Drains? What do you mean?' asked my friend.

'Not in the literal sense. Not the variety of heat exchangers designed to transfer thermal energy from one medium to another for the purpose of cooling and heating. Nor the one that is an exit point for waste water,' I said.

'Yes, yes, I know that.'

We then went into a discussion about how interacting with some people energises us, and interacting with some drains us. Hence, the term "Radiators and Drains".

Radiators are the people who fill you with energy. You feel happy to see them. You feel good talking to them. You look forward to interacting with them. When you part from them, you feel good about yourself. A little more loved. When you think of them, you look forward to meeting them next. They are fun to be with, positive, upbeat and full of life. They need not necessarily be your friends. They can range from the clerk at the post office, or the courier delivery boy, or the guy who delivers newspapers, or the mailman, or that co-worker who you never got around talking to, or that classmate who is more an acquaintance than a friend. The only parameter for people to be classified as radiators is that when you finish interacting with them, you feel happy, positive and recharged.

Drains, on the other hand, leave you feeling down. They may not say anything unpleasant, but after talking to them, you feel completely drained out. Your enthusiasm levels dip. You are vaguely dissatisfied, but unable to put a reason to it. Drains might have talked very politely and pleasantly to you, but after interacting with them, you feel somewhat inadequate. You feel, as though, something has been taken away. Again, a friend or a relative might be a drain. Drains are not necessarily people whom you hate. They could be just anyone in your life who leaves you feeling inadequate in a way that cannot be described.

My friend added that Drains could also be called emotional vampires. She said when she was younger, it was a big problem for her because she always wanted to take care of people, make them feel better, help fix their problems… It took her a while to realise that they really don't want help. Most just want your undivided, constant attention and the only way they are going to feel better is after they've brought you down to where they are.

Another friend took the analogy further. He said that he has also met Fridges (cold people who left you chilled), Baths (people who are so welcoming that they make you want to dive in and soak up in the situation they are creating), and even Chemical Toilets (they're full of crap). He added that he once knew someone who was a cross between a food processor and a waste disposal unit!

The older I become, the more certain I am of what I want. I know now that I do not want to waste my time with the "Drains". There are many beautiful, positive and uplifting things in life. There is so much beauty, so much joy. Life is short and fleeting. It is entirely up to us to enjoy each moment.

There will, of course, be days when you feel sad, hopeless, and despondent and as though all is lost. When that happens, it is time to pick up the phone and call the best Radiator you know.

Family or career?

Sometime back, for the promotions of one of my novels, we ran a campaign on the social media pages called "Ask Preeti". The readers could ask me whatever they wanted, and I would answer one oft-asked question each week.

One of the questions that I keep getting asked is: should we choose between our passion or family? You are very successful in managing both – family and work. What should one do? How do you manage both?

Here is what I think.

Family is the basic unit from which we start our life. What we learn from our families helps us deal with different social situations. In a way, it is the family that is providing us the "blueprint" to our personality. We then grow up, get a job and start our own families.

I don't think there can ever be a perfect work-life balance. At any given point of time, you will always be tugged by both. I know, because I have faced it. I have even given up an important literature festival that I had to attend, as it clashed with my daughter's graduation ceremony. Another time, I did not attend a parent-teacher-meeting, as I had a deadline to meet. It is always a tug between my writing and spending time with my family. Even though I try to keep the weekends completely free, sometimes it becomes impossible, as some work comes up. There might be a journalist calling with a tight deadline who wants my input. Or my newspaper editor might request an extra column that I need to write. Or there might be a prestigious lit-fest that I simply cannot refuse.

I weigh my options for each particular project and then decide whether to accept or refuse.

When my children were much younger, I chose to give up my corporate career as I wanted to be around for them. Now they are much older and hence independent. I had no doubt in my mind that it was the path I wanted to take. But if you ask me whether it was easy, I would say it most definitely wasn't. Back then, when I made that choice, I gave up my economic independence for a while. I was not very happy about that. However, I threw in my all into parenting. I looked for options that would allow me to be home when my children came back from school, as I wanted to spend time with them while they were growing up. I took up full time writing only when they were older. There was no guarantee that I would meet with success. However, I was fortunate that things turned out well.

When you make a choice, you have to ask yourself these questions:

1. How important is it for you to earn well?
2. How many hours of work do you have to put in to sustain your current/desired lifestyle?
3. Are you the primary bread-winner of your family?
4. How important is it for you to be able to spend time with your family?

Once you answer the above questions, you will be able to make a clear choice.

As for me, if you were to ask me whether I would choose my passion or my family, I would definitely say family. But if this very family is going to hinder and stand in the way of my passion (I am very fortunate to have a supportive family), then I am clearly going to be unhappy. In that case, I would take a call and choose that which gives me more contentment. Only if we are happy can we make our loved ones happy.

We owe it to ourselves to take care of our own needs first. Only then can you give your hundred percent to your family as well as your passion. And if your career is your passion, then you have hit a jackpot!

Writer's high

Most runners speak of a 'Runner's high'– that endorphin rush you feel when you have been involved in strenuous activity, leading to a feeling of euphoria and happiness. Yesterday I hit a writer's high. It was something I have never experienced before. I wrote 7,256 words yesterday. That is the highest ever number of words I have written in a single day, in my entire writing career.

I patted myself on the back. And when a friend pinged to ask how the writing was going, I said, 'Super, I hit a writer's high today. This is the highest number of words I have written in a single day in my entire life.'

'Wow. Keep rocking!' he typed back.

But I don't think he understood why it meant a great deal to me.

Writing a book is *a lot* of work really. You have to think of a story (a completely original one which no one has done before, which by itself is a mammoth task), a plot, characters (they have to be likeable, believable, and people who you can relate to), dialogues, what happens to them. You have to write coherently. But more than anything, you have to discipline yourself to sit at the computer all by yourself and type out word after word after word. Day after day after day. It is a L.O.N.E.L.Y. profession.

You have to be involved with people and interested in them and understand them, empathise with them, yet be strangely detached, to be able to write.

There is no one really to check your progress and nobody you are accountable to. So that makes it that much more harder. You can take a year, two years, even five years to finish a book. It is so entirely up to *you* and *you alone*.

I have my own ways of pushing myself. Sometimes I compete with fellow authors who are working on a book. We ping each other at the end of the day and ask, 'WC?' (WC stands for word count. There is great joy in typing 2,300 or 3,200 or whatever the number of words one has written. A sense of satisfaction of a day well spent.)

Sometimes I tell a friend (whom I am dying to meet) that I will go out with them only when I hit 'x' number of words. Then they keep checking as to how many words I have written so that we can go out.

I report my progress to my children and spouse and the house-help as well as my dog. They are the only ones who actually care about my word count. Or rather, they are the only ones who will listen to me. (Oh, and that friend too who I promise to go out with, on completing 'x' words.)

Most full length novels have a minimum of 60,000 words.

This is how it is classified:

500–1,000 words – Flash story
1,000–10,000 words – Short story
10,000–40,000 – Novella
40,000–60,000 – Novelette or "Novel Lite"
60,000 and up – Novel

156 • *Preeti Shenoy*

Yesterday I crossed 60K words of the book I am working on. (Which was when I hit the writer's high.)

'Oh, so does that mean the book will be out soon?' asked the friend.

'No! The real work starts now!' I replied.

Most people do not know that once a manuscript is complete, and a publisher is chosen, it takes a minimum of 4-6 months for the book to be out.

The manuscript goes through the first revision. The structural changes if any, are suggested to the author. The author then incorporates the changes or convinces the editor about why the changes should not happen.

Then begins proofreading.

The first round is done and the manuscript comes back to the author. Generally it looks like a war-field with all the corrections in red looking like blood-wounds. I winced when it first came. I kid you not.

Then the corrections are made and sent back.

Each coma, each full stop, each word, is examined over and over.

Then the second round of proofreading happens.

Then the third.

Sometimes fourth and fifth. (I have proofread till the words begin blurring and I fall asleep in front of my laptop.)

We squabble about fonts. About an exclamation mark. About a word repeated.

Every single detail counts.

Then the cover.

And the book title.

And the acknowledgements.

And the chapter titles.

And how it should all appear in the final version.

And finally it is a BIG moment when the book gets an okay and goes for printing. For my last book, up to the last moment, we were making changes. It is something like a rocket-blast off – the frantic holding-of-breath till it takes off.

The tension doesn't end there.

When you finally hold the book in your hands (the much-coveted author copies), it is truly a moment that makes me weep.

Every single time.

No matter how many books you have written, it is still the same.

Welcome to the writer's world.

It is a lonely place, a crazy place, a place which makes you hurtle down into depths of despair when you can't get those words out, but at the same time, a place which makes you soar higher than even the heavens when things go right.

Epilogue
How this book came to be

Life has a way of unexpectedly pulling the rug from under your feet. Till it happened to me, I always thought that these are the kind of things that happen to other people. These are the kind of things that happen in Bollywood movies. These are the kind of things that you read about and hear about. It can never happen to you.

Yet it did. Healthy people don't drop down dead for no reason. Usually.

But September 7, 2006 was not a usual day. Well, it seemed like a usual day to start with. My husband was travelling and was in Delhi, which was not unusual. The kids had gone to school, which was very usual. Home after school, they expressed the desire to eat pizza, which was again not very unusual. I agreed to take them to a nearby pizza joint, which was again not unusual.

They had a friend playing with them and I took him along as well, after seeking permission from his mother, as it would seem rude to ask him to go home. The children loved the outing. We were all busy munching pizzas and having a great time, blissfully ignorant and unaware of something that was happening in another part of the world. Something that would shatter my faith in my friends, would transform my outlook towards life, and would change me completely as a person.

We came home and the child who was playing with my two went back to his house. I put the children to bed early and called up my husband, saying that I was doing okay, and wanted to sleep early, as I was very tired and asked him not to call me (when he is travelling he usually calls, and we chat about our respective days) and went to bed.

At 10:30 pm the phone rang. It was my husband. He said my dad was dead. I couldn't believe what I was hearing.

'What? What?' I yelled. My brother who was in Mumbai, had been informed and he had called up my husband. They decided that it was best that my husband told me first.

I was in a daze. I did not know what hit me. I think, when something like this happens, we go into a denial mode to cope. My dad's and mom's tickets had been booked to come to Pune (where I had just moved to) at the end of that very month. My brother's wife was expecting their first baby and was eight months pregnant. My dad had no illnesses which people his age suffer from and not only that, he was also remarkably fit for his age. He had even scheduled meetings for the next day as he was actively involved in many things. Besides, he was just 66 – which was not an age that could really be called "old age". This just could not be happening.

I had to set out for Kerala (where my parents lived) immediately. My husband managed to arrange for a reliable taxi through his office contacts. There are no direct flights from Pune to Kochi. It was decided that the children and I would go to my brother's place in Mumbai.

My brother's wife, in her advanced stage of pregnancy, could not travel and so we decided that we would leave my kids with her, and my brother and I would fly to Kerala. My brother managed to get tickets from Mumbai to Kochi by the 5:00 am flight for both of us.

My children, then aged eight and five were very close to my dad. I knew instinctively that it would be too much for them to bear. It would be best if they did not accompany me.

It was around 12:30 am, in the middle of the night, that the cab arrived. My children were fast asleep. I asked the cab driver to carry the sleeping children into the cab, one by one. I remember throwing a few clothes into my bag, and packing another bag for the kids, in a complete daze. It takes about three hours for the journey from Pune to Mumbai by road. In between, my kids woke up and asked where we were going. I burst into tears and told them that their grandfather wasn't well and that their uncle and I were going to see him. (For the last time, I did not add.) Then I swallowed my tears quickly and pretended to be brave because I did not want to worry them.

I remember being incredibly calm when we arrived at my brother's house. I think we were both in total denial. Two close friends of my brother had arrived and stayed with us that whole night. We were talking about various things and even laughing and joking, as though it was just a normal everyday thing. I think it was our way of coping.

Even on the flight, the gravity of the situation did not hit us. I remember feeling like it was a big adventure. I jokingly told my brother to eat up whatever they gave us on the flight as we would not be able to eat for the next 24 hours. We discussed various relatives whom we had not seen for ages ever since we left Kerala.

Once we arrived, it was a completely different scene altogether. There was a crowd of people waiting outside the picturesque cottage where my parents lived. Everyone was waiting for our arrival. I threw my bag outside and ran to my mom. She hugged me and let out a loud wail. I was stoic and comforted her. My brother had to go and bring my dad's body from the mortuary. That moment in time when they pulled out the body from the freezer and he saw my dad's frozen legs, is something that is etched deep inside him, he says. My dad – who was so jovial, loud, positive, inspiring and a towering presence in our lives – was now just a dead body with a number tag attached.

For the next seventeen days, my brother and I stayed with my mom. There was a continuous stream of visitors. My dad was the kind of person who would chat up everyone and would be completely at ease with everyone – right from the watchman to the head of a multinational company, and even ministers and politicians. He had to meet people from all walks of life in his line of work and always struck a chord with them. Dad always believed in helping others and in fact, after retirement, had started a trust and did a lot of social work to help the aged who were poor, abandoned or neglected. It is a registered trust called Society for Welfare of Aged and Poor and is now run by my mother.

My father used to also hold these English conversation classes to teach the village kids to speak the language, and it was free of cost.

People came from all over the country to pay their last respects. Usually, it was dad who did all the talking whenever someone visited. Dad loved to talk, and mom, my brother and I were just shadows. He would carry on the conversation and interact with visitors while we would just sit back and be entertained. My brother and mom are not much of talkers and so naturally, the onus was on me to converse with the people who called upon us. I think it was one of the toughest things I have ever done in my life.

On the one hand was my grief, my shock, my anger, my pain. All I wanted to do was curl up and be by myself. I was emotionally very close to my dad and my dad adored me. Everything I did was perfect in my dad's eyes. We would speak to each other on the phone almost every day, and even the previous day I had spoken to him. Each thing in that house reminded me of my dad. I hated it. I wanted to scream. I wanted to die. I wanted to just talk to him once more. I wanted to yell out that this was bloody unfair and I wanted to tell everyone to disappear. I wanted my dad back.

Of course, I could not tell all this to the people who were visiting. I could see they were hurting too. Some of them openly wept and told us what my dad meant to them. I ended up comforting them.

I was on autopilot. I remember rattling off the sequence of events in the order in, which they had occurred. I was able to completely isolate my emotions and appear stoically calm as I narrated to the visitors, for what seemed to me like the hundredth time, the way he died, how he had had his dinner, how he was watching TV with mom, relaxing in his easy chair and how he suddenly stopped talking. He had closed his eyes and was gone. I could say it all in detail without the slightest trace of regret or pain in my eyes or on my face. Everyone said I was incredibly brave. I had to be. It was the only way I could hide my pain. It was the only way I knew of coping.

We brought my mom back with us. She would stay with my brother till his wife had the baby. I don't think we even remember the air tickets that had been earlier booked for mom and dad. Does a person dying count as a no-show passenger? We didn't bother to find out.

After I returned home to Pune, life for my husband and children resumed as usual. The children had their school to go to. My husband had to go to work. I had not yet resumed the workshops on thinking skills that I did for children at that time. Also, I was emotionally in no state to do so. I remember feeling so alone. For days, I could not sleep. Each day when I woke up, the first thought that would occur to me was that my dad was no more and it was like someone had slapped me hard. I would often break down and my children and husband got very used to it. I didn't feel like going out anywhere, yet. I so badly wanted to talk about it to people.

People don't know how to respond when someone talks about death. There is usually an uncomfortable silence. Most people don't even want to hear. That was a shattering discovery that I made. Till then I had had so many friends. I was jovial, funny, smart and great fun to be with. But when this happened, people were seeing a different side of me for the first time. They saw my tears and they saw my pain. I was totally broken when I discovered that people who usually talked to me were now avoiding me completely. One friend told me, 'I am not ready to talk about this. Please don't tell me anything.' I could not believe it. This was a friend I used to chat with, laugh with and have hours of fun with, when things were fine. For the first time, I realised what a naive fool I had been. People wanted me only because I was a source of amusement, an entertainment to them, not because they really cared. For the very first time in my life, I realised that not everyone who laughs with you is a friend.

I remember waking up and functioning like a zombie, sending my kids to school and after my husband left for work, I would log on to the internet, desperately wanting to talk to someone about my pain. Most of my friends said things like 'You will get over it', 'May his soul rest in peace' and 'At least he did not suffer'. Then they suddenly went offline. Laugh and others laugh with you; cry and you cry alone. I was rapidly discovering that this much-used idiom is indeed true.

I was sick of crying in front of my kids and my husband and I began putting up a happy face in front of them. How long could they keep comforting me? My husband was extremely supportive and was always ready to listen. But I felt bad to think that every day when he came home from work, he would find me in tears. It is not easy to deal with a person who is weepy all the time and who had turned into someone completely the opposite of what she used to be.

In a desperate attempt to remain sane, I began painting – a hobby that had taken a back seat for a while. I also started to blog. I joined a social networking site and made new friends. One particular person whom I met online (and whom I have never met in real life) helped me a lot. He had just quit his job and was on his way to join a college in the U.S. He had a couple of months before he joined. He would chat with me for hours. He would also call me up and we would talk. We would have long conversations and they helped.

I also met an artist from the UK (whom I later met in real life when I travelled to London) with whom I began exchanging mails. He too had seen pain (he had lost both his parents and a child) and the mails he used to send felt like he was reading my mind. He understood fully my grief, my anger, my anguish. He gave me strength, as did my other friend. I shall never forget their kindness and I am so grateful that they came into my life at that point of time.

Then I began writing. Apart from the internet, my pieces found their way to magazines and newspapers. It was cathartic. Little by little I was limping back to life. I now realised how fragile life could be and we really have to *grab* it and live without regrets. I realised the value of being healthy and the value of having one more day to live.

My feelings were reflected in my writings and lots and lots of people began writing to me saying how what I wrote had given them hope, how it had changed their outlook and how much it had helped them be positive. Many encouraged me to put it all in a book and what you are holding in your hands is the result of that.

I hope you enjoyed reading it, as much as I enjoyed compiling it.

Live, love and laugh. The gift of life is worth cherishing. If you want to do something, do it right now. Don't put it off. If you love someone, tell them, show them, and express what you feel. Live without regrets and cherish the gift of laughter and life.

Every single moment of it.

✸